# THE WORLD OF THE RUFFED GROUSE

# LIVING WORLD BOOKS

John K. Terres, Editor

# THE WORLD OF THE RUFFED GROUSE

*With Text and Photographs by*
Leonard Lee Rue III

J. B. Lippincott Company
*Philadelphia and New York*

U.S. Library of Congress Cataloging in Publication Data

Rue, Leonard Lee.
    The world of the ruffed grouse.

(Living world books)
Bibliography:  p.
1.  Ruffed grouse.  I.  Title.
QL696.G2R83         598.6'1        72–748
ISBN–0–397–00817–1
ISBN–0–397–00913–5  (lib.  bdg.)

*To*
*the memory of*
*my sister Virginia*

# Contents

# THE WORLD OF THE RUFFED GROUSE

# Author's Introduction

THERE ARE MANY who claim that the ruffed grouse is the king of the game birds; and almost no one disputes it. The hunted bird not only deserves respect, it commands respect. The sight of a ruffed grouse is enough to quicken the beating of the heart, and the pursuit of this bird requires more effort, more persistence, more knowledge, more luck, and a greater expenditure of shot shells than does any other type of bird hunting. It also causes more excitement, more aching muscles, more missed shots, and probably more cuss words. Those who do not shoot grouse but seek it out for joy, study, or photography don't fare much better. Just what manner of bird is the ruffed grouse? I have only a camera and a pen, but I shall try to describe it in this book.

I have been a neighbor to the ruffed grouse for most of my life because I, like the grouse, have always lived on the fringe of the forest. My study of the bird was unavoidable; our paths have crossed often. In our area, at any given time of the day, at any given time of the year, I can go forth and usually locate grouse.

This book is an outgrowth of a lifetime of absorption. Never content with just my own observations and always willing to learn from others, I have pursued information about the ruffed grouse wherever I could find it. I have unhesitatingly appropriated the vast amount of research and study done by those listed in the bibliography and hereby acknowledge my indebtedness to them.

I have also been most fortunate in having many friends and associates who have helped me, either directly or by letter, in acquiring a greater knowledge of the ruffed grouse. My heartfelt thanks go to Carl Ahlers, G. A. Ammann, Rod Amundson, Dan Armbruster, John C. Baird, Manny Barone, Hope Sawyer Buyukmihci, Kenneth Chiavetta. Ben Day, Bud Disbrow, Roy Erie, Newton Kingston, J. Burton Lauckhart, William Longeley, Ed Miller, Bill Mullendore, Walter L. Palmer, Edmund J. Sawyer, Roy W. Trexler, Joe Taylor, Neil Van Nostrand, Earl A. Westervelt, Frank Woolner, Wally Wrede, and Thomas J. Wright.

Many things improve with age, but my handwriting does not happen to be one of them. My very special thanks and appreciation go to my sister, Evelyn Rue Guthrie, who not only can read my writing but is willing to convert it to a typewritten form.

*Blairstown, New Jersey*                    LEONARD LEE RUE III

# Meet the Ruffed Grouse

It was always exciting to watch old Roy Erie light his kitchen stove. After opening the damper, he would throw several handfuls of fine split kindling or dry corncobs into the firebox. A can of kerosene—"coal oil," Roy called it—always sat in the corner behind the stove. After pouring a liberal application of kerosene on the kindling, he would put the center stove span and rear lid back in place and toss a lighted wooden kitchen match into the front stove hole. The resultant *ka-foooom* would shake the stove, rattle the lids, and threaten to tear the stovepipe loose from the chimney. But the fire was going.

This was all pretty exciting fare for a boy nine years old who had been born in the city and raised there until his folks bought a farm, near Belvidere, New Jersey, up on the hill above Roy's place. But then many things about Roy were exciting. I must call our neighbor "Mr. Erie," my folks insisted, but Roy would have none of that. His father had been Mr. Erie, he said, but Roy was his name and that was what I should use. I think he was the first adult I ever called by his first name.

Roy always knew what would interest a boy, and on different occasions he would open the wall cupboard and bring out a cardboard box that to me was a treasure chest. There were pieces of arrowheads and even a few whole ones, long curving incisor teeth

*A female ruffed grouse tail, fanned.*

from woodchucks, penis bones from exceptionally large raccoons, walnuts that had been cut open by squirrels, and a few feathers, birds' eggs, and other knickknacks. He also had the first tails of ruffed grouse that I had ever seen, spread out like fans.

Roy didn't call them ruffed grouse; he said they were the tails of "mountain birds" or "partridge." The tails had come from birds that had fallen to his old double-barreled shotgun. It was a few more years before I found out that "mountain birds," "partridge," and ruffed grouse were all the same.

The ruffed grouse is the most widespread nonmigratory game bird in North America and has more than a hundred localized or colloquial names, among them American partridge, common partridge,

*Many people may be "ruffled,"*
*but the grouse—never.*

birch partridge, partridge, pa'tridge, pat, mountain bird, mountain cock, mountain pheasant, pheasant, carpenter bird, tippet, thunderwings, drummer, fool hen, woodpile quawker, white-flesher, shoulderknot ruff, and even rough grouse. The Indian tribes of North America also had as many names for the ruffed grouse as there were tribes and dialects. But no one except the most misinformed person calls the bird a *ruffled* grouse. Many people, particularly hunters, may be "ruffled," but the grouse—never.

Many of the names given to the grouse were descriptive of its actions or were misapplied by the early colonists who were influenced by similar European birds with which they were familiar. (Our word grouse may come from an Anglicized version, "grous," from the French words *greuce, greoche, griais, griesche,* meaning "spotted bird.") The bird was known to the Europeans from the earliest days of exploration and settlement. Hernando de Soto's secretary recorded in 1540, while the expedition was in what is now South Carolina, that "a chief sent two thousand Indians loaded with rabbits, partridges,* cornbread and many dogs, but only two wild turkeys."

In 1584 Sir Walter Raleigh sent out two ships from England to Virginia. Among the crew was Robert Beverly, an historian. Beverly reported seeing wild turkey "of an incredible Bigness, partridge, pigeons, deer, rabbit, fox, raccoons, bear, panther, elk, wildcat, buffalo, possum, wild hog."

Carolus Linnaeus first described the ruffed grouse in his *Systema Naturae* of 1766, from one sent to England by John Bartram in 1750. Linnaeus designated the bird's scientific genus name as *Tetrao,* and the species, or specific, name as *umbellus,* because of the bird's ruff, which could be erected like an umbrella. In the 1810 edition of

---

* Partridge was a misapplied name for the ruffed grouse much used by early New England settlers. The grouse is not a partridge but belongs to the grouse family Tetraonidae, of which there are about eighteen species in the world. True partridges belong to the pheasant and quail family, Phasianidae.—*The Editor.*

Shaw's *General Zoology,* the zoologist J. F. Stephens changed the generic name from *Tetrao* to *Bonasa,* the name we recognize today. (*Bonasa* is derived from the Latin word for bison, suggesting that the grouse's drumming is like the bellow of a bull bison.)

A ruffed grouse is a small chickenlike bird, ruffed and partly crested, its color varied with rufous, black, and gray, with a dark band on the tail, and with tail and wings of equal length. It is quite different from other North American grouse, such as the blue or dusky grouse, the spruce grouse, Franklin's grouse, and the ptarmigans.

In my contacts with wildlife I am always measuring, weighing, and probing everything I can get my hands on. The following data are

*Blue or dusky grouse* (Dendragapus obscurus).

from a female grouse that I collected (shot) on November 15, 1969, in northwestern New Jersey.

Overall weight: 21 ounces
Overall length: 17¼ inches
Overall wingspan: 22½ inches
Overall single wing length: 10 inches
Overall leg from body to sole of foot: 6 inches
Overall toe length: 2¾ inches
Overall bill length: ⅞ inch
Overall tail-feather length: 5½ inches
Overall crest-feather length: 1¼ inches
Overall ruff-feather length: 2½ inches
Number of wing feathers: 10 primaries, 15 secondaries

My reason for singling out that particular grouse is that it was the largest female I have ever handled. The adult female ruffed grouse in autumn ordinarily weighs from 17 to 21 ounces with the slightly larger male weighing between 20 and 24 ounces and having an overall length of 17¾ to 20 inches. Adult grouse of either sex weigh more than their counterparts among that year's young birds. Although 20 ounces is about the average weight for an adult male grouse, a

*Spruce grouse* (Canachites canadensis).

*Franklin's grouse* (Canachites franklini).

*Willow ptarmigan* (Lagopus lagopus).

*White-tailed ptarmigan*
(Lagopus leucurus).

number of males attain weights up to 28 ounces. There are cases of even heavier weights. A grouse killed near Hornellsville, New York, weighed 32½ ounces; another in Rutland, Massachusetts, weighed 33 ounces. The record and still champion, so far as I can find, is the bird killed by John Burham in the Adirondack Mountain region of Essex County, New York, that weighed 36 ounces.

I speak of telling the male from the female grouse as if anyone could do it, and actually anyone can, once he knows what to look for. Whereas in many species of birds the difference in the coloration, size, and external appendages makes differentiating the sexes of that species very easy, this is not true of the ruffed grouse. However, there are many characteristics by which one can distinguish between the male and the female grouse; even if most of them are not always dependable, they are usually accurate enough to be used with confidence, and observing a combination of most of these characteristics makes an identification as to sex fairly certain.

The male ruffed grouse is slightly larger than the female and has a chunkier body and larger head and ruff. The feathers on the male's crest are usually over 1½ inches long.

Both male and female ruffed grouse have a small bare-skin patch right above the eye. The female's patch is a bluish-gray; the male's may vary from light salmon to bright orange, especially during the breeding season. The female appears to have a rounder, plumper breast, but this is because her ruff feathers are not as long as the male's feathers, which make his neck appear larger, with the ruff feathers growing down in a straight line beneath his bill.

The flank feathers of a female are basically white with distinct black bars; the male's flank feathers are beige, buffy on light tan, with irregular brownish bars.

The wing feathers of the male, and the wings themselves, are slightly longer than those of the female; the difference is apparent even when the wings are at rest and held against the body. The tips

*Ruffed grouse (Bonasa umbellus). The male is on the left, female on the right. The male, which weighs more, has a heavier head, a chunkier body, a longer neck ruff that extends across his chest, and longer wings that extend farther back. The eye patch is visible above his eye. The female has broken chest-line markings and a white belly, while the male has a dark belly. The male's tail should be longer; here the tail length appears to be the same.*

of the primary feathers of the female extend just to her rump, while those of the male are longer and extend beyond his rump.

With the bird in the hand, most hunters immediately fan the tail and check the subterminal band, which is the first wide black band, to see if the black is continuous. Most males have an unbroken black band, while most females have a band broken by brown on the two center rectrices (tail feathers). The additional narrow black bands on the male's tail are much more distinct and more sharply delineated than those of the female.

The black band, however, is not as accurate an indicator of sex as is the measurement of the actual length of the two central tail feathers. To measure the tail-feather length, you do not need to pluck the feathers but can measure them right from the flesh. Measured in this

*Here the male is on the right and the female on the left. The ruff feathers on the male are longer.*

way (which doesn't spoil the tail fan), center tail feathers with lengths of over 5¼ inches are considered to belong to a male; lesser lengths indicate that the bird is probably a female. The most accurate measurements are those taken of plucked feathers and measured right to the tip of the shaft. Those more than 5⅞ inches are male; shorter ones are female. The longest tail feathers that I have in my collection are slightly more than 8 inches.

After fanning the grouse's tail to check the black subterminal band,

*Ruffed grouse tail fans. Note broken dark band on the female's, at top.*

the hunter may spread the tail to a full 180 degrees for another check on its sex; the feathers of the male's tail will spread in a semicircle without the feathers separating, while those of the female usually fail to overlap.

Gordon W. Gullion and William H. Marshall, investigating Minnesota ruffed grouse, reported that one of the two center tail feathers is as positive an identification of an individual grouse as a fingerprint among humans. They found that the design or pattern of shed feathers matched the replacement feathers identically. (Their research was carried out on banded birds, making such identification positive.)

The actions of the ruffed grouse can also be used to determine sex. Although both sexes have been seen to strut, no female grouse has ever been known to drum and no male will hatch out eggs.

Nature does occasionally produce exceptions, or aberrations. Since most or all of the foregoing characteristics are diagnostic, the last resort in making a positive identification of the sex of a ruffed grouse

*The author, fanning a male grouse tail 180 degrees.*

is an internal check of the gonads. In the male, the two testes are attached to either side of the backbone in the body cavity just behind the rib cage. They are blue-gray and each about the size of a small pea during the hunting season. The slightly larger egg mass (ova) of the female is in the same area and is usually yellow-red.

A ruffed grouse is basically brown with lighter underparts and a mottling of dark bars, darts, or arrow points. Some people think one can tell the sex of a grouse by its color because grouse are dichromatic and are found in either the so-called red or rufous phase or the gray phase. The two colors are not an indication of sex, however (the male or female may be either red or gray); color appears to be linked to environmental moisture and the altitude and latitude at which the birds live. (Dichromatism is common in such other types of wildlife as the screech owl, fox squirrel, and, to a lesser degree, the great horned owl.)

The two color phases are most evident in the tails of the grouse, although the ruff is sometimes also affected. Most of the time the grouse's ruff feathers are jet black, with a metallic green or purple iridescence. In the darker red phases, the ruff may be reddish brown or even a deep chocolate color.

In my area of New Jersey, both phases seem to be found in one brood, irrespective of sex or location. Or are they? I have taken both red and gray birds from the valley as well as from the ridge top of the Kittatinny Mountains, yet my neighbors Chet Kimble and Bill Pitman of Bevans, New Jersey, have always claimed that the red birds were valley birds while the grays were mountain birds, and both of these men have shot far more grouse than I ever will. Scientific investigation seems to bear them out, and yet it is a fact, although seemingly contradictory, that both red and gray birds will occasionally be found in the same brood.

Taxonomists, concerned with the scientific classification of the ruffed grouse, have described the general coloration of the ranges of

28

*In the fall, the male's testicles—indicated on either side of the knife tip—are the final proof of sex.*

*This female ruffed grouse in Quebec is a grayish-brown color.*

various subspecies in *The Check-List of North American Birds,* fifth edition, 1957. For example, ruffed grouse in Central Alaska are the grayest of all; birds in the rain forests of Washington are a very dark rufous color; in the aspen groves of Utah, grouse are the palest red, and the brightest red grouse are in the southern Appalachian Mountains. The grouse I saw so frequently in my seventeen summers in the Quebec wilderness area were a grayish-brown, the same color type that I see in New Jersey. The simplest way of stating it is that red-phase grouse are more common at lower elevations, in drier areas, and in southern regions; gray-phase grouse are more common at higher elevations, in wetter areas, and in the more northern regions.

Recent studies by Gullion and Marshall on ruffed grouse in the Cloquet Forest Research Center in Minnesota highlight the relationship of color to survival. They reported that during a winter when the snow is deep enough for the grouse to burrow into it, red-phase grouse have a survival rate as high as gray-phase grouse, but that when this snow cover is lacking, gray grouse have a much higher survival rate. They also noted that an examination of 3,320 ruffed grouse tails from known areas all over Minnesota revealed that gray-phase grouse are more numerous in the evergreen areas of the north while red-phase grouse predominate in the hardwood stands in the southern part of the state. They noted that the gray color blends with the dead needles and coniferous forest duff, while the red color better matches the dead leaves of the hardwood forest floor. Such protective coloration is a tremendous survival factor.

This finding fits a general rule of grouse distribution, but the interesting feature is that as the conifers are cut down or burned off, even in the northern areas, red-phase grouse become dominant.

I want to repeat that—although the gray-phase grouse is considered the bird of the more northern, wetter, conifer-covered, heavier-snow, or higher elevations and the red phase is considered a bird of the more southern, drier, hardwood-covered, or lower elevations—both color phases can be found, however rarely, in the same brood, irrespective of sex or location.

Almost every form of living creature is subject to albinism. Lacking coloration, the hair, feathers, or scales are white. Ruffed grouse are no exception to this phenomenon, but the condition is exceedingly rare. A partial albino grouse, having a white breast, belly, throat, neck, legs, and some wing and tail feathers (the rest of the plumage was normal), was shot near Fort Kent, Maine, and Sidney Wiswall of Ballston Spa, New York, shot a pure albino ruffed grouse near his home.

I can find no record of melanism, or all-black coloration, in the ruffed grouse.

The feathers of birds perform many important and varied functions. As the bird's external covering they help maintain its body heat and temperature, which in the ruffed grouse averages 107 degrees Fahrenheit. The feathers assist the grouse in flight, provide protection against rain, and, as already mentioned, provide camouflage protection by their coloration.

Feathers do not grow in even distribution on a bird's skin; they grow in patches, known as feather tracts, with bare skin areas between them. Feathers are of many sizes and shapes and are controlled by subcutaneous muscles. During the famous New York State study reported by Gardiner Bump, Robert Darrow, Frank C. Edminster, and Walter F. Crissey, a researcher plucked and counted the feathers of a female ruffed grouse. There were 4,342.

Most birds have feathered legs and a bare tarsus—the straight part of the foot, immediately above the toes and commonly called the "shank." On the ruffed grouse, however, these leg feathers continue down the front of the tarsus, or shank. Unlike turkeys and pheasants,

*The ruffed grouse's coloring proves an effective camouflage.*

32

grouse do not have a spur growing from the tarsus, but they do have special adaptations of the feet that enable them to walk on soft snow. Ruffed grouse develop scales—comblike processes called pectinations—on the outside of each toe, which act like snowshoes, and the ptarmigans—grouse of the Far North—have their entire foot and toes covered with hair feathers that serve the same purpose.

A ruffed grouse usually has eighteen feathers in its tail, which are prominently displayed by the male during courtship. The tail is also used for balance and to provide lift and steering control when the bird flies. The ruffed grouse is not a sustained-flight bird; the short, broad, cupped wings are adapted for its typically limited, powerful bursts of speed. The grouse has ten primaries—the long flight feathers of each wing. These grow out of the outer, or "hand," part of the wing.* It also has fifteen to seventeen secondary flight feathers in each wing, which grow from the next inner section corresponding to our forearm or ulna. The primaries are stiff, which in flight helps produce the "thunder" of takeoff; however, a grouse can also fly almost silently when it wishes, or at least with a minimum of sound.

The ruffed grouse has been clocked at a top speed of fifty-one miles per hour over a measured course, although its average swift flight is about forty miles an hour. Its startling takeoff and evasive actions in flying through heavy cover make it appear to be going much faster.

A grouse usually flies only when forced to. It prefers to walk from place to place, taking advantage of all possible cover. I don't believe I ever saw a grouse fly for more than a quarter of a mile. As any hunter knows, a grouse has white breast meat while a duck has dark breast meat. This means that the grouse does not have the rich supply of

---

* A bird has almost complete control over the "hand" section of its wings, just as a man has over his hands and fingers. During the evolution of the bird wing (from a lizardlike ancestor's "hands" or front feet), two of the finger bones fused into one; the others have disappeared.—*The Editor.*

*The rock ptarmigan* (Lagopus rupestris) *in summer . . .*

*and in winter. The feet are feathered year round.*

*Ruffed grouse take short steps, placing the feet directly ahead of each other.*

blood capillaries and oxygen in its flight muscles that the duck has, and needs, for its sustained flights; a duck's red flight muscles also have more myoglobin and readily oxidized cytochrome than the grouse's white ones.

The distance that a ruffed grouse can fly is of great interest to biologists, and some interesting observations and experiments have been made. Most grouse researchers believe that one mile is about the limit that a ruffed grouse can fly with one takeoff. To test this theory, Walter L. Palmer of Michigan took live-trapped wild grouse out in a boat and released them over water. No bird flew more than a quarter of a mile, but the birds were undoubtedly confused, probably never having flown over water before. Palmer took this into account by commenting that all of the birds flew slower than expected; two of the grouse took off again after landing on the water, and one flew farther the second time than it did on its initial flight. As a grouse's feathers are not waterproof, there is no way of knowing how long they could have stayed afloat if they had not been picked up.

*36*

Palmer realized that his tests could not be conclusive, but how do you make a grouse exert itself so that it will fly its maximum distance over land? He concluded from his observations that a ruffed grouse could not fly more than a mile in a single flight.

On the other hand, P. A. Taverner, a Canadian ornithologist, believes that the ruffed grouse on Grand Manan Island (which lies six miles off the coast of Maine in the Bay of Fundy) flew there, since there are no records that man introduced them to the island.

Ruffed grouse, like other birds, may be subject to defects at birth and still survive. Chester Kowalski of Altoona, Pennsylvania, for example, found a full-grown grouse in good health that wasn't going to fly anywhere; it had been born with just one wing.

Under normal conditions, the heart of a ruffed grouse beats about 342 times per minute; its average breath rate is 63 inhalations per minute. Both of these rates are speeded up or reduced by the various external factors and conditions to which the grouse is exposed.

Going back to my record card of that large female ruffed grouse, I have some interesting internal measurements. The bird's esophagus from the mouth of the crop was about 4¼ inches long, and her crop had only about two tablespoons of food in it. The largest crop content

*A ruffed grouse crop, stuffed with grass, fruit, and leaves.*

measurement that I can find is 153 cubic centimeters. I measured this amount and found that it is almost 5 ounces, or a little more than half a cup. I once had a crop, from a grouse taken in the winter, the contents of which were all that I could hold in my hand, at least a cup of material. Unfortunately I did not measure it.

The crop of the bird is used as a storage compartment, corresponding to the rumen of a deer. It serves the same purpose, allowing the bird to feed quickly and then digest its food at leisure in protective cover.

Below the crop is another short piece of esophagus, measuring 1¾ inches long, that leads to the gizzard. The gizzard is the powerful muscular stomach, about 1½ inches in diameter and ⅞ inch thick, which grinds the food into pieces small enough to be passed on for digestion. To aid in the crushing process, the grouse picks up small stones, called grit, which are retained in the bird's gizzard to help it grind its food.

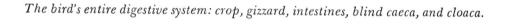

*The bird's entire digestive system: crop, gizzard, intestines, blind caeca, and cloaca.*

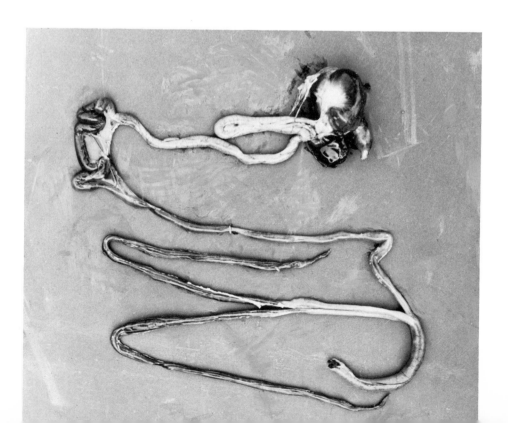

From the gizzard, food passes through the duodenal loop and the large and small intestines, where the digestion and assimilation of food takes place. The distance from the gizzard to the vent is 42 inches. The two caeca, which act as a blind gut, separate the small intestine from the large. Each caeca is 18 inches long and is gray, with longitudinal gray-green stripes.

All birds have a single body opening called the cloaca through which pass the bird's excretions and, in copulation, the male's sperms.

With the exception of the turkey vulture, most birds, grouse included, apparently have a deficient sense of smell. The grouse has good eyesight, however, and notices the slightest movement made by anything in its immediate area. It also has a keen sense of hearing and is as alerted by sound as it is by movement. The grouse also has a wide repertory of utterances (vocalizations) used to communicate with other grouse. They chirp, coo, squeal, peep, hiss, and perk; and all of these sounds have many variations and inflections.

The ruffed grouse has a potential life span of about six years, although it rarely realizes its potential. As is true with most of our birds and other animals, the bulk of the ruffed grouse population is killed or dies each year. A grouse that holds the longevity record of eleven years, however, was reported by Wallace Grange.

The ruffed grouse population is also controlled by a ten-year cycle, so that the population fluctuates widely from year to year and area to area.

The ruffed grouse is adaptable. The coming of the white man to this continent forced many changes upon the bird. In many places the grouse no longer exists, largely because its habitat has been altered or destroyed; on the other hand, in many places the grouse is more plentiful now than at the time of European colonization.

In different parts of its range, the ruffed grouse is seemingly a paradox. In suburban or rural areas, where the hunting pressure is great, it is the wariest bird imaginable. In some wilderness areas,

*The ruffed grouse soon learns to be wary of man.*

however, where the grouse has perhaps never seen a man, the bird still lives up to its nickname of "fool hen." Such birds, letting their curiosity get the better of them, may sit in a tree until they are knocked down with a stick.

Fossil records of birds are relatively scarce because the bones are lightweight and fragile, are easily and quickly destroyed, and rapidly decompose unless they are in protected places. The bones of ruffed grouse have been found in Frankstown Cave in Pennsylvania, Cumberland Cave in Maryland, and in Potter Creek Cave in California, among the bones of extinct forms of a crocodile, an eland, and some giant peccaries. These bones have been dated back to about twenty-five thousand years ago, during the latter part of the Pleistocene period. Those grouse lived at a time when modern man had taken the first strides down the path to dominance over all of the world's creatures.

No one disputes that the future of the ruffed grouse is in man's hands. But many other animals have vanished while the grouse is still holding its own. That's what I mean by adaptability.

# Spring

SPRING'S ARRIVAL is only a date on man's calendar, but in the out-of-doors it is a promise of better days to come.

In a tangled thicket festooned with old grapevines, a large male ruffed grouse sits immobile, his brown feather pattern providing excellent camouflage against the leafy floor of the woods. The grouse fed before the wind gained momentum and he will feed again when it has diminished. But for now all his needs have been met, and the bird sits still—at least, outwardly—but deep within him are faint stirrings that the grouse perhaps does not even recognize. He will respond to them, however, as these urgings make themselves felt more strongly with the passage of each day.

The internal time clocks of all living things are sensitive to the amount of daylight available, and each creature reacts physiologically, according to its kind. So the male grouse instinctively responds to internal drives that are ingrained in his species. Despite the weather, the grouse knows it is spring.

The male ruffed grouse is strongly influenced by territorialism, an urge to have a plot of ground that he will defend against all other male ruffed grouse. Weather, food, and cover may dictate changes in the range and habits of each individual, but in the spring of the year, all the males will establish themselves in the available territories. The territory held by each male grouse depends upon many factors,

*43*

but the age and the strength of the grouse are most important.

Being a homebody, a member of a nonmigratory species, the male ruffed grouse will seldom range more than a quarter of a mile around the center of his activities. The home territory is neither round nor square but takes its shape from features of the topography or from boundaries imposed and recognized only by the grouse himself. Males more than one year old will occupy the most desirable territories or move in to take over better ones vacant since the previous spring. The younger grouse have the less desirable ranges, according to their status, and acquire their territories in the fall right after the dispersal of the young birds of the year. About 8 percent of the males leave their territories after they have established them, but in doing so they are acquiring a better area left vacant by the death of a formerly dominant male.

Probably the most commonly known fact about all male ruffed grouse is that they "drum" in the spring. This drumming serves to proclaim territorial rights, challenge rival males, attract females, and provide an outlet for exuberance. The drumming "log" may be the focal point for a male grouse, but it does not necessarily have to be in the center of his territory.

Research has shown that where food and cover are plentiful, approaching optimum conditions, the ruffed grouse population may increase to four males per square mile in the spring. (There are many more grouse than that per square mile in late summer if the breeding and rearing seasons have been successful.) All studies seem to substantiate the fact that the environment will not support (or the grouse themselves tolerate) more than four males per square mile in the spring, and there are seldom that many.

When the winter's snow has finally receded and the bare patches of earth begin to warm up, the flowering stalks of bloodroot, hepatica, anemone, and trillium push upward, forming a stage setting for the

*Old apple orchards are ideal territories for ruffed grouse, for they provide both food and shelter.*

drumming log. (Although we have referred to it as a drumming log because a log is chosen about 95 percent of the time, the ruffed grouse male may also choose a rock, anthill, stone row, stump, or even a bare patch of earth.) Not just any log is used. The preferred log is huge, old, and moss-covered, with the root structure still attached, usually the trunk of a tree that has fallen naturally, although, as long as it is almost level, it can be the trunk of a tree that has been cut down. It may be sound, rotten, or hollow. It is usually more than twelve inches in diameter.

*45*

*Hope Sawyer Buyukmihci's photograph of a ruffed grouse drumming, taken in 1968. The first photograph of drumming was taken sixty years earlier by her father, Edmund Sawyer.*

*Spring*

When a ruffed grouse drums, his message is intended for any grouse that may be within hearing, but in effect he is announcing his presence to the entire world. At all times a grouse is aware of danger from predators, but especially so during the drumming season.

The male ruffed grouse prefers a large-diameter log because it provides greater elevation, allowing him to see farther. He prefers open hardwoods because they are leafless in early spring, and he can more easily see anything that moves nearby. Apparently he distrusts large evergreens in the area because they are favored perches for hawks and owls that may, at times, be his greatest enemies. He prefers that some saplings provide overhead coverage, to foil the attack of the raptor when it comes. (This is also why he likes the tree roots sticking up on one end of the drumming log.) He also likes saplings or under-brush at one end to mask his own arrivals and departures. He favors a southern exposure because such slopes provide more of his required cover and food.

Just as a grouse recognizes and responds to these conditions, so can you recognize them when you look for drumming logs. Not that

*A fine ruffed grouse drumming log.*

you won't find drumming logs in other places, because you will. There aren't enough ideal spots to go around, and therefore some grouse, meaning the lower-status ones, must use north slopes or leave much of the hill country empty. The last two drumming logs I found were on the north side of a hill. In south Jersey I have seen drumming logs surrounded by very heavy brush, and in Quebec I have found them in areas where there were no other trees except conifers or the "needle" evergreens such as hemlocks, pines, and spruces. The grouse have to make do with what exists.

Recognizing a drumming log when you see one is easy, particularly if it is being used. The most notable sign will be the collection of the bird's droppings. Biologists figure that a ruffed grouse voids four droppings per hour. One log had 1,116 fresh droppings on it, which would indicate that that particular male had spent 279 hours or more on his log. The droppings are not scattered over the log but are deposited carefully in one spot.

Drumming logs also show signs of wear, particularly those covered with moss. As a grouse usually drums from exactly the same place each time, the moss will be worn off and the wood will be brighter in such spots, and the powerful sweeps of the wings in drumming will fan the leaves away so that the bare earth is exposed around the log.

*Fresh droppings most easily identify the drumming log.*

*Spring*

The male's attachment to his drumming log—or logs, because he may have several—is very strong. Often he will continue to use his favorite one even if the forest around the log becomes drastically changed. Many logs have been used continuously, by successive generations of grouse, over long periods of time. If their logs are less than ideal, however, about one third of the males will abandon them for others within their own territories.

When a male ruffed grouse acquires a territory formerly held by a rival male, he usually appropriates the drumming log, too. Studies made in Minnesota prove that this can be a fatal mistake; some predators recognize that an hereditary drumming log is a good spot to catch a meal. On the other hand, the grouse are especially alert when drumming; using banded birds, the study brought to light the startling fact that any male grouse that changes drumming logs each year within his own territory automatically doubles his life expectancy.

Ruffed grouse may drum at any time of the year and at any hour of the day, but the regular drumming season starts in March, peaks in April, and declines in May. As a rule, most drumming starts before dawn, continues until 7:30 A.M., and then tapers off, being sporadic if at all during the daytime, with another peak of activity in the late afternoon and evening hours. During overcast periods the grouse seem to drum more or, perhaps because it is overcast, they drum more continuously through the day when they are more likely to be heard. However, some grouse drum much more than others; each grouse is an individual, and the times of drumming are decided by each bird.

Moonlit nights will find some grouse actively drumming all night. Harlan Metcalf, a professor at Cortland State Teachers' College in New York, told of a grouse he observed that drummed only at night but did so all night long. The grouse would start to drum about 9 P.M. and performed once every five minutes all through the night before retiring at 6 A.M.

*49*

I suspect that some males sleep on their drumming logs. It's a sure fact that most of them are exceedingly early risers; even if you arrive at a log at 4 A.M., you may find the grouse there ahead of you.

For years there was argument and speculation about how ruffed grouse produce the drumming sound. High-speed film, high-speed cameras, and the extremely high speed of electronic flash finally proved conclusively how the drumming is done.

The male usually approaches his drumming log very stealthily, often under cover of darkness. After gaining the log, the grouse seems to feel he has made it "home safe" because he discards all caution, usually parading up and down the full length of the log, as if to inspect it, and flicking his tail. When he struts during this inspection, his wings droop until they touch the log, his tail is raised almost vertically and fanned 180 degrees, his head is brought back, and the ruff is elevated until it looks like the umbrella from which his species name derives. Resembling a miniature turkey cock, the male ruffed grouse is now the epitome of wilderness splendor.

Selecting some spot that is perhaps slightly raised near the larger end of the log, the grouse turns his body sideways to the length of the log. If he has used this log previously he may turn about several times, peering here and there as if deciding upon some new spot or direction but invariably facing the same direction from the exact spot he previously used. If the log lies on a slight slope, the grouse will face downhill.

Placing his feet as carefully as a sprinter using starting chocks, the grouse stands with the body perpendicular, pressing his tail against the log. The wings are extended backward as a man would do in stretching. A few single beats are given, and then the wings begin to flash—faster, faster, faster—until they become a blur, slowing down again to stop in about ten seconds. The first beats sound like hand claps and the accelerated strokes sound like the rolling beat of a muffled kettledrum or distant thunder, with the sound becoming

*The male approaches his log very stealthily.*

less loud as the wing action increases and dying away as the wings are brought to rest.

The sound of the drumming is actually a sonic boom made by the wings beating the air. John Madson described it as an implosion, caused by air rushing in to fill a vacuum created by the flashing wings. The wings are brought forward, bending inward and upward at the same time. The pinions are widely separated during these strokes, much like the slats of an opened Venetian blind. Because the air is being spilled or foiled through these slats, the bird is able to remain standing in one spot instead of becoming airborne. The grouse probably creates almost as much pressure with his wings on the back stroke as he does on the forward sweep. Although the feet are carefully placed, the grouse frequently raises his body so that the tail is no longer braced against the log, which proves that there is no propelling force in the wings.

Other birds can also make sounds by beating their wings against the air, but only the grouse has developed the ability to drum.

The grouse usually sends out his muffled drum roll about once every five minutes, for as many hours as he cares to do it. At the conclusion of each drum roll, the grouse gradually relaxes and smooths his feathers down and peers intently all around. He not only is apprehensive of danger, he is anticipating a rival grouse and ready for a receptive hen.

Occasionally he hops off his log and disappears into the brush. There he may peck at the ground and feed a bit, preen himself, or perhaps doze for a while. When the urge moves him he comes back to his log, and again his challenge rolls and reverberates throughout the woodland.

Although the sound of a grouse drumming is loud and carries well, it is very difficult to pinpoint; a distant-sounding grouse may actually be much closer than one that sounds nearby. (The sound is of such low frequency—40 cycles per second—that it seems no louder when

*The great horned owl is one of the grouse's natural enemies.*

the drumming grouse is two hundred feet away than at six hundred feet.) A person with normal hearing can detect a ruffed grouse drumming a quarter of a mile away, or more if conditions are favorable.

Predators, having ears far superior to ours, must be attracted to the grouse by its drumming, yet this apparently does not put the grouse at a disadvantage. The great horned owl is one of the grouse's natural enemies and is most active during the dark hours of dawn and twilight when much drumming takes place. Yet the owl very rarely kills a grouse drumming on its log. This was a puzzle until Albert Brand of the Cornell Laboratory of Ornithology discovered that the owl cannot hear the grouse's drumming. The owl's hearing range is in the higher register; * it can pick up the squeaks of the mice and rats it feeds upon but the grouse's drumming range is too low for the owl to be able to hear it.

The drumming of the ruffed grouse has often been likened to an old one-cylinder gasoline engine. Evidently it sounds that way to a grouse, too, because many males will respond to the sound of an engine—or anything else that produces a low thumping noise. For example, grouse may be drawn to farm tractors being used in the woods or in fields near woods. In Buttzville, New Jersey, a farmer named Pritchard had such an experience. A male grouse came out to the sound of his tractor and eventually allowed Mr. Pritchard to pick him up. The reactions of grouse to engines vary. Some birds are very aggressive, flying at and attacking the machines and the men driving them; others seem to want to make friends of the machines and the men and become very tame. Some of the grouse continue such friendships over a period of years and appear whenever the machine is started.

Woodcutters have often experienced the same friendships. The

---

* According to one investigator, the range of hearing of the great horned owl is from 7,000 to a low of 60 cycles a second—the owl is apparently incapable of hearing lower frequencies of sound (for example, 40 cycles a second).—*The Editor.*

steady *chock-chock-chock* of their axes is attractive to the grouse. Jonah Howell is a man to whom I was introduced by, or really because of, a grouse. Jonah worked in the Jenny Jump State Forest in New Jersey. One day while poking holes in the earth around the base of some old apple trees, to fertilize them, he was attacked by a male ruffed grouse. The grouse evidently took the thumping sound made by the punch bar as a challenge and rose to meet it.

When Jonah did not fight back, the grouse assumed he was the victor and with true magnanimity adopted Jonah. Over succeeding days the association continued, and finally the grouse allowed himself to be picked up, stroked, and hand fed. The fame of this friendship quickly spread and a good friend of mine, John Stuart Martin, took me to meet Jonah and Sam, the grouse—for so he was named—and to take photos. Sam adopted as his territory an area through which almost every female visitor to the forest had to pass on her way to the comfort station. He gradually became very tame and would pick at food thrown to him by the campers, but his allegiance to Jonah remained. Only Jonah could pick him up.

Some male grouse are very aggressive. Carlyn and Bob Galati, friends of mine from California, were walking on the La Salle trail in Minnesota's Lake Itasca State Park in the middle of May in 1955 when a disturbance in the bushes bordering the trail caught their attention. Out of the underbrush stalked a male ruffed grouse. He made a constant clucking sound while fluffing up his feathers and erecting his crest, ruff, and tail. As Bob stepped forward, the grouse dashed over, grabbed his right pants cuff, and proceeded to shake it like a terrier worrying a rat. Then the grouse stepped back as if to view his handiwork. When Bob took another step, the grouse returned to the attack and again wildly shook the pants cuff. Bob is a wildlife photographer and wanted to record this action on film. He asked Carlyn to walk past him. The grouse proved to be a real gentleman; although he would walk alongside Carlyn, he would not

55

*Jonah Howell and friend.*

peck at her. But when Bob attempted to move, the bird repeated the attack.

The grouse followed them to the parking lot. As the Galatis got into their car, the grouse noticed his reflection in the shiny hubcap. This drove him into a frenzy and he attacked his reflection. When Bob began to move the car slowly forward, the grouse flew up on the hood and fought his reflection in the windshield. As Bob picked up speed, the grouse flew to the ground and chased after the car on foot. This entire procedure was repeated each time Bob and Carlyn visited the area over a period of the next two weeks.

The reactions of male grouse on their drumming logs to outside stimuli are as many and varied as the number of grouse observed. All are exceedingly wary of danger from natural predators, but their reactions to man, particularly photographers, are always unpredictable, as just shown—except during the hunting season.

Most photographs of grouse drumming are taken from bird blinds, either close to the drumming log, so that the bird can be photographed directly from the blind, or at a distance by remote control.

If the grouse is on the log before the photographer arrives, it may flush when disturbed and not come back. Or it may flush and within a short while come back and resume drumming. Albert G. Shimmel of West Decatur, Pennsylvania, located a very cooperative grouse already drumming on the log when Shimmel arrived in the early morning darkness. When the grouse stopped drumming Shimmel thought that he had left, so he turned his light on the log. There in the glare of the spotlight sat the grouse; and there he remained. Shimmel entered his blind and got everything set up. As if that were the signal for him to begin, the grouse again started to drum and continued until midmorning.

My luck doesn't work like that. I flushed a grouse off a log one dark morning and he never returned. That is, he didn't return to the log I was covering from the blind. In frustration I heard him do roll after roll from another log somewhere in the vicinity.

One time when Edmund J. Sawyer was working in a blind, the grouse refused to use the log in front of the blind but used another nearby. Using his fists, Sawyer pounded on the ground in imitation of the grouse's drumming, and the male immediately responded by returning to the log in front of the blind. Another photographer got the same results by beating on his chest with the flat of his hands.

When Fred Everett and Clayt Seagears were working on the New York State grouse investigation (Bump *et al.*), they put a tame male and female grouse in a small pen out in the woods so that they could take photographs and make sketches of the male drumming. The grouse performed beautifully; he drummed on the ground, from a rock, and on a log. Once, when the men moved the log, the grouse flew up on Everett's back and settled to drum. At the last moment, however, he apparently changed his mind, and so was lost what surely would have been a most unusual incident.

We humans may not be able to tell the sex of a particular grouse, but neither can another grouse. The male's drumming amounts to a prime-time television commercial. By his drumming he advertises to rival males that they are trespassing if they step upon his territory; he is also telling the females that he is available as a mate.

If another grouse appears in the vicinity of the drumming log, the drummer jumps off the log, fans out his tail, droops his wings, erects his crest, and slowly struts toward the other grouse. When the two birds are about fifteen feet apart, the male will lower his head and rush at the newcomer, stopping just short of actual contact. With head and neck outstretched, he will rotate his head rapidly from side to side, hissing loudly all the time, trying to intimidate the other.

If the new arrival is a female she will probably ignore the threat gesture and demurely start to feed. A rival male will meet threat with matching threat. The two may peck at each other, each trying to grasp the other with his beak. If one is successful, he will shake his head rapidly, creating a painful bite. Or, like game cocks (although they have no spurs), one grouse will jump into the air and try to knock over his opponent. In addition to pecking and kicking, they also use their wings to flail away at one another. Seldom is the fight prolonged; the weaker male soon gives way and runs or flies out of the area. Usually the resident male is the victor. He has two distinct advantages: he is defending a home territory, and if the rival were larger or stronger he would already have a territory of his own and not be still trying to acquire one.

Ruffed grouse are usually thought to be monogamous, although in captivity one male will breed with as many as five hens. In the wild, a male seldom has such opportunities, but he will breed with one or more females if they move into his territory.

While the male is drumming, displaying, or fighting, the female seldom pays much attention to him. Then there comes a period when the male seems to realize that such rough and high-handed tactics are getting him absolutely nowhere. At this calm stage the male grouse follows the female around, pecking at the ground and then gently at the base of her bill. In this mood the female accepts his advances and copulation takes place, but only when she is ready.

After copulating, the male again becomes aggressive, perhaps even more so than before. His belligerency takes the form of almost continuous drumming, strutting, and posturing. Although the male considers his drumming log his personal property, other forest dwellers don't recognize his rights. Such animals as red and gray squirrels and chipmunks all use the log as a highway. During this period the grouse may even challenge the rights of other animals to use his log. As the month of May passes, however, so does this madness.

Meanwhile the hen is concerned mainly with preparations for her forthcoming family. A site for the nest has been chosen long before breeding takes place. Every nest I have ever seen has been against the base of a stump, tree, or clump of bushes, preferably against a stump or tree. It is as though the female feels safer when protected from one side. (Of course such an obstacle can also be to a predator's advantage because it provides a screen to mask its approach.) And every nest I have ever found has always been adjacent to, or close to, an old wood road, path, or forest clearing. For a long time I thought that perhaps I found nests in such places because I was more apt to walk there than through the underbrush. However, extensive studies made of ruffed grouse in forest areas, where all of the acreage was systematically covered, came up with similar findings, so we must conclude that the female grouse greatly favors such spots. During the brooding period, the hen will also need access to water to drink, because she does not have the time to gather dewdrops as she normally would.

The nest itself is little more than a slight depression in the leaves on the forest floor. I have never seen any evidence of nest construction other than the natural molding of the nest's shape by the female's body. The few feathers found in the nest are, I believe, the result of normal molting and not a deliberate placement.

It has often been claimed that the female ruffed grouse hides her nest even from the male because the male will break the eggs in order to prolong the breeding season. So far as I know, no one has investigated this statement, but I can give no credence to it. It may be true that the male may not know where the nest is located, but that is only because females have much larger ranges than males, about a mile across, and the nest may be outside of territory that the male considers his.

The female usually lays an egg a day until her clutch is completed. Eleven eggs are considered average, although there may be as few as eight eggs or as many as fifteen. On the rare occasion when eighteen

*A female ruffed grouse on her nest.*

*This nest is in a thicket.*

or more eggs are found in a single nest, it is usually because two hens have used it. Carl Ahlers, a friend of mine from Columbia, New Jersey, located a grouse nest that contained twenty-two eggs. It wouldn't be impossible for one hen to lay that many. A biologist who was testing the laying ability of a ruffed grouse removed an egg a day from her nest, and she laid thirty-six eggs before she quit. There have also been records of a hen pheasant laying eggs in a ruffed grouse's nest.

The hen usually lays her egg early in the morning, sneaking in and out of the nest to do the job. Then she will move out of the nest area and spend the rest of the day feeding or consorting with the male. Only after her clutch has been completed will she begin to incubate the eggs so that the embryos within them will develop and hatch.

*Spring*

Food is always important to a bird or any other animal, but especially to the female during the period when she is laying her eggs or producing her young. These functions put a drain on her body and may affect not only the adult but the unborn young. If food has been plentiful and the female is in good health, the chances of her offspring's survival are greatly enhanced. A female that has been deprived of the proper amounts and kinds of food may not have young at all or will produce young that do not have the vitality needed to survive.

Exhaustive studies show that the ruffed grouse has an extremely varied diet, feeding upon more than six hundred species of plants, insects, and other animals. During the spring 98 percent of the ruffed grouse's diet is vegetable matter. The birds are still feeding upon buds and newly sprouted leaves of aspens, birches, cherry trees, and apple trees. They also eat the evergreen leaves of sheep sorrel and mountain laurel. Newly green leaves of the wild and barren strawberry, clover, dandelion, partridgeberry, and wintergreen are avidly sought. Burgeoning fern sprouts are important foods, as is the continuing supply of Christmas fern. Having almost unlimited food

*Christmas fern is almost always available as food.*

*Nine eggs is a smaller than average clutch.*

sources, therefore, most grouse usually lay good sets of eggs with a high degree of fertility.

The eggs of the ruffed grouse are a brownish buff, with occasionally some light brown spots. They are about 1½ inches long and a little more than 1 inch in diameter. The egg laying begins in April and early May, but unseasonably cold weather may delay the process by preventing ovarian development in the female.

Ground-nesting birds such as grouse are subject to a greater amount of danger than those that build their nests in shrubs or in trees. The span of egg laying and the twenty-four-day incubation period is a time fraught with danger for both the female grouse and her eggs.

It has been claimed that the female ruffed grouse, in an effort to camouflage her eggs, will pick up leaves with her bill and place them on her back while she sits brooding her eggs. When she is flushed from her nest, the leaves are said to drop down and cover the eggs. I don't know how much of this is true, but I have seen grouse with leaves on their backs, and every nest that was vacated had at least a couple of leaves on top of the eggs. The leaves could have been blown there by the air motion created with the hen flew off the nest, but no matter how they got there they were there.

The New York State study had 548 ruffed grouse nests under observation. Of those nests 59.4 percent hatched out successfully while 40.6 percent were destroyed by predators. This is a very interesting fact because studies of *all* types of birds and their nests, including songbirds, show the same 60–40 percentages. Nor should the 40 percent of the nests that were destroyed be counted as a total loss, because usually the female grouse will make a second attempt at nesting, although the second clutch of eggs will probably be smaller in number than was the first.

*A ruffed grouse nest destroyed by predators.*

*The lynx is another of the ruffed grouse's natural enemies.*

In addition to hawks and owls, other predators will take either the female or her eggs or both, if they can. Dogs, cats, opossums, skunks, raccoons, foxes, coyotes, wolves, weasels, minks, fishers, martens, bobcats, lynx, cougars, and bears are all on the list. Nowhere in the ruffed grouse's range are all of these predators about, but some of them are present, at times, in parts or all of the grouse's range.

Predation upon ruffed grouse—or upon any other animal—is very complicated. Sometimes the amount of predation may depend on the availability to predators of "buffer" species. If there are large numbers of mice, rabbits, or hares that predators can feed upon, or may even prefer because of their relative ease of capture, predation on grouse will be light. When such buffer species are scarce, the predation on grouse may be higher, especially if the environment in which the grouse live is not "secure" or of good quality. And if the grouse are suffering from disease, predation will be high.

In the New York State study, conducted through the 1930s to the mid-1940s, it was found that skunks and foxes were responsible for breaking up many grouse nests. If comparable studies were made today, the raccoon and the opossum probably would head the list, because these animals are more plentiful than they were thirty or forty years ago and are now more numerous than skunks or foxes.

0

*Raccoons and opossums probably take more grouse now than foxes and skunks.*

*While the red squirrel will eat grouse eggs, the chipmunk only plays with them.*

However, if predators do not skim off some of the grouse, other factors will. Diseases, predators, and weather are only a few of the more obvious but built-in natural controls that take some grouse at all times, thus keeping the population within the capacity of the environment to support it.*

Some animals take only the eggs of the grouse. Both red and gray squirrels will take grouse eggs but the red take more, because grouse are more frequently found in the same habitat as the red squirrel.

Chipmunks, too, eliminate some grouse eggs, but they don't eat them; they usually roll the eggs out of the nest and play with them or else hide them under the leaves.

* Entire books have been written about the complexities of predation, a subject which can only be touched on here. We recommend especially *Of Predation and Life* by Paul L. Errington and the chapter "Varmints" in *Our Wildlife Legacy* by Durward L. Allen. Both of these books are listed in the Bibliography.—*The Editor.*

*Spring*

Snakes, particularly the black racer, pilot black, pine snake, and fox snake, will all eat eggs and can swallow an entire grouse clutch at one encounter. On the other hand, through most of the summer snakes consume enormous numbers of mice, ground squirrels, and other rodents that compete with the grouse for seeds and other plant foods.

One action by the female grouse remains a puzzle to the biologists. After a week or so of brooding her eggs, she will discard any that are infertile by rolling them out of the nest. How does the hen know which egg, or eggs, are infertile?

Weather plays a very important role in the success of the brooding hen. If it is abnormally cold, the hen, which is on shortened food supply because of her brooding requirements, may become weakened. If the weather is hot and dry, brush or forest fires may scourge the woodlands and, if not killing the hen, will surely destroy the eggs.

In 1883, E. A. Samuels found a grouse nest in an abandoned crow's nest. Evidently that was one mother grouse which became tired of having other animals consider her and her eggs their lawful prey.

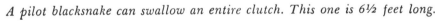

*A pilot blacksnake can swallow an entire clutch. This one is 6½ feet long.*

# Summer

SUMMER IS A TIME of excesses, of superabundance beyond comprehension. Not all births come in June, but although many of the birds, mammals, reptiles, amphibians, and fishes of the temperate zone give birth or hatch their eggs before or after June, it is still the one month when these living things the world over reach their greatest numbers.

As dawn rises slowly, the ruffed grouse hen becomes increasingly agitated. For twenty-three to twenty-four days she has incubated her eggs, sitting closely on the nest, leaving it only once or twice each day for a short period of time to feed and to seek water. Upon returning, she has invariably turned each egg before commencing to brood again. The short periods of time that the female was off her eggs did them no harm. Now she both hears and feels the pecking of the chicks in their shells beneath her breast. It starts off with a single tap, and then another, and another. In response to the code tapped out by the first chick the other chicks begin to peck at their own imprisoning shells. The hen gets off the nest and nervously walks around it, flicking her tail, clucking, and *putt-putt*ing, then returns to continue her brooding. The sound of the hen brings forth a renewed effort from the chicks, and in a short time the eggs begin to move and roll about and then to crack and be thrust apart. The hen takes no part in the proceedings beyond giving vocal encouragement and interrupting her periods of brooding.

*71*

Each baby bird is equipped with an egg tooth that is attached to the front tip of its upper mandible. This egg tooth is a holdover from the sharper egg tooth of snakes, the young of which are born with an egg tooth that they use to slit the leathery shell. The birds make good use of their egg tooth even though their eggshells have a higher calcium content and are more rigid than are those of the snakes.

Prior to hatching, the baby will rock its head back and forth, back and forth, cutting a groove in the shell. When the bird is ready to emerge from the shell, it pecks at this weakened area until it cracks. Sometimes the shell will be punctured completely around the large end. Then, using its body like a hydraulic jack, the bird slowly forces the shell apart. While the chick is hatching, it is moving or turning in its shell, because the bill and feet may alternately be seen through the crack in the egg.

The job of opening the shell is a drain on the chick's energies, and it alternates its periods of activity with periods of rest. The time that elapses from the first pecking until the chick emerges from the shell varies from one or one and a half hours to as much as seven hours.

Grouse eggs at the time of hatching weigh about ½ ounce; at hatching the chick weighs little more than ¼ ounce. As the chick finally forces off the large end of the shell, its apparently naked head appears. The down on the chick is wet and is not discernible, but the ten primary and fifteen to seventeen secondary feathers show as small, dark, wet strings.

The chick flails about with both its feet and its wings after hatching, which appears to aid in the drying of the down and the feathers. The eyes, which were closed at hatching, start to open in about ten minutes and are wide open and bright in fifteen minutes. The chick's movements slow down and finally almost cease as it dries, which takes about half an hour.

While the chick is resting, it assumes basically the same position that it did while in the egg, only now the head can be stretched out farther.

*Ruffed grouse chicks all hatch the same day and are dry and fluffy in half an hour.*

The chick lies with its head upon the ground and with both feet alongside its head. Within perhaps twelve hours, the entire clutch has hatched.

While the young are hatching, the female warms the chicks by sitting very lightly on the eggs. To brood tightly as she had formerly done would restrict the chicks' activities and hamper the hatching. Part of the time, instead of actually touching the eggs, the hen will hover above them, shielding them and retaining their warmth.

This is the most critical time in the life of the ruffed grouse, and adverse weather is probably the most important factor controlling the population. If it is raining the hen will straddle the nest and, using her body and extended wings as an umbrella, shield the emerging chicks from the elements. Records show that her efforts are not always successful; a wet, cold season during the hatching period definitely precedes a localized low grouse population in the fall.

The peak of the hatching season is in the latter part of May and the first two weeks of June. At that time, the sex ratio is in favor of the female, usually by about 51 percent to 49 percent or more. The ratio becomes inverted with the passage of time.

Young grouse are precocial; within a short time after drying off they are ready to leave the nest. While the female was brooding the eggs, her inactivity decreased the amount of body scent that she gave off, providing her with additional protection. The chicks are practically odorless, and predators have difficulty in finding them. However, the eggshells do have an odor and the hen is anxious to leave the nest and the shells behind, so, as soon as the last hatched chick is dry, the entire family leaves the nest, never to return.

Baby grouse do not have to eat at once (though they usually do) because they have varying amounts of unused yolk left in their stomachs. This yolk is slowly consumed over the next three to five days. During the next ten to twelve days insects provide the bulk of the food consumed by the babies. It is only during this period that any-

*Just like a domestic hen, the mother grouse covers her chicks with her wings until they are old enough to roost in trees.*

thing other than plant life is important. The chicks vitally need the high protein that insects provide.

Baby grouse are exceedingly alert and respond instantaneously to anything that moves. If the object is small, such as an insect, the chick snatches it up and eats it. If the object that moves is large, the chick will usually "freeze" by remaining motionless.

While less than twenty-four hours old, the chicks can walk, hop, and run, and they attempt to fly by fluttering their wings. Their eyesight is keen and they can easily see an aphid or a tiny spider moving on the underside of a leaf. Many times I have seen them snap up an insect that I hadn't noticed. They often jump up off the ground to snatch an insect from a leaf. They eagerly chase ants and eat them. Grouse babies are constantly on the move, a powerhouse of energy.

As I mentioned earlier, all of the nests of ruffed grouse that I have ever found were at the edge of a road, a path, or a woodland. The important word in that sentence is "edge"; in fact, it is the cornerstone of any discussion of ruffed grouse. Important at all times, it is doubly so when hatching and rearing the young.

An edge is just what it implies, a place where one type of environment meets another—for example, where the forest meets the fields. An edge is a break in the continuity of any vegetative type, a place where sunlight can foster new growth, possibly unrestricted growth. It is this growth which produces the greatest variety of plant life and offers the greatest possible variety of food and cover.

Forest fires can be very destructive. If the fire is extremely hot, it will destroy all plant life and much of the animal life (or drive it away) and perhaps even the humus of the forest floor. But fires can also be useful to wildlife. If the fire is not too hot, and many are not, it may kill the standing trees and perhaps some of the under-growth, but the potash created by the fire is a valuable fertilizer. With the tree canopy opened, the sunlight can again get to the forest floor

*One-day-old ruffed grouse chick.*

to promote the growth of a new cycle of plant life.

A fire is the starting point in plant succession. Roots that have survived the fire, seeds that can germinate only after exposure to fire, and seeds deposited in the area by the waste products of wildlife—all find such forest clearings ideal, and within a year much of the clearing will have a ground cover of plants. An area of this type may cover a few acres or thousands of acres, but where it borders on other types of land—woodlands, open fields, pastures—it is still known as edge.

Selective cutting or lumbering will do the same thing on a smaller scale. We all hate to see a beautiful forest cut, to see the monarchs dragged out and sliced into logs. Yet in many ways a mature, or climax, forest often provides homes for a minimal number of wild things because it has no understory of small trees, shrubs, and grassy openings. Indiscriminate lumbering, or clear-cutting, is worse, as it desolates the area; however, small or limited clear-cut plots in the forest will soon produce more wildlife than before, because of the increased number of edges. It is a matter of values. What do we want, unbroken forests or managed forests that produce more and greater varieties of wildlife? It seems to be a matter of what type of land management is decided upon. If it is wildlife management, especially to produce more grouse, it is the diversity of habitats and the amount of edges that count.

Nature moves inexorably, over many years, through plant succession, toward a climax—that is, the climax or ultimate forest that is in balance with soils and climate. If the succession is interrupted by fire or man, the process starts all over again.

The fields of abandoned farms begin to grow wild in a single year. Unhampered by the restrictive forces of plowing or the shearing and cutting blades, it is freed from the renewal of farm crops. Many weedy annuals begin to show vigorous growth, and perennial herbaceous plants stake out their claims upon the open land. Not only do all types of saplings and shrubs extend from the woodlands, along the edges of the fields, but invading "pioneering" trees such as aspens, alders, and birches claim open ground as far as the wind can carry their seeds. All of this creates different habitat types and edges. The combination, in juxtaposition to old orchards, overgrown pastures, and new sprouted woodlands, creates an ideal habitat for ruffed grouse chicks, and these are the spots the females now seek out.

In the grassy areas the young find grasshoppers, crickets, harvestmen, locusts, beetles, cutworms, leafhoppers, earthworms, inchworms, ants, and aphids. Within ten days the chicks are picking at green plants and soon change over to the almost straight vegetable diet they will follow for the rest of their lives. The adults gorge themselves with the fruits of strawberry, blueberry, blackberry, bunchberry, raspberry, and partridge berry. They also eat seeds and plant parts of jewelweed, sedges, clover, violets, grasses, buttercup, smartweed, fungus, pussytoes, ferns, and others.

Life is fraught with danger in many different forms for the young of most species. A rainy season not only chills the grouse chicks but turns every hole or rut to a death trap into which the little ones may fall. A dry season holds the risk of fires that may sweep through an area like a flash, destroying all but the most mobile animals in its fury. Against such hazards the grouse mother has no defense. Her instincts and wiles are best used against predators.

As a mother grouse convoys her charges through the high grasses and bushes, she keeps up vocal utterances designed to keep the chicks

*A forest reclaiming old fields makes good grouse habitat.*

from straying. The chicks are intent upon food: they chase an ant here, jump up to snap at a fly there, pick an aphid from a leaf, and pause to slake their thirst with a glimmering drop of dew. The hen, always alert to danger, feeds and utters soft *puk-puk-puk* or *putt-putt-putt* sounds, which the chicks answer with *tsee-tsee*. (Female grouse chicks are much more vocal than the males.) As long as the chicks hear this *putt* sound, they continue to go their way, clambering over roots, running around stones too high to jump up on, and searching constantly for food.

At the first sight or sound of anything that could be danger, the mother's call changes to *preeent-preeent*. The alarm is instantly heeded. With a flurry of action the chicks seek shelter. Their mottled brown coloring provides excellent camouflage, and they disappear from view as if whisked off by a tornado.

If the danger should be a raptor, the hen usually flushes wildly from the spot, flying a short distance and then diving into heavy cover. Usually the sight of the hen is enough to deflect a hawk's attention from the chicks to herself.

Ben C. Robinson once saw a red-tailed hawk that would not be fooled like this. Instead, the hawk landed and began to search for the young in the high grass. Immediately the mother grouse flew back and landed nearby. Instead of showing the customary fear, the grouse approached the hawk and ran in little semicircles in front of it but just beyond its reach. Much preferring a large grouse to a small one, the hawk tried to capture the mother, but the high grass hampered the hawk's wings and talons and its progress was most awkward. The smaller, sleeker grouse was in her element and delayed the hawk until her chicks had all vacated the immediate area and hidden themselves. Her duty completed, the hen then sought shelter for herself, leaving the baffled hawk no recourse but to seek its dinner elsewhere.

To decoy four-footed enemies away from her chicks, the female usually feigns injury. Predators, ever alert for ill or crippled prey,

*The mother grouse's vocal sounds change when danger approaches.*

are easily led from the area where the chicks are hiding. For slower animals the female will walk or run along, dragging her wing and crying piteously. To keep ahead of larger, faster animals such as foxes, she will fly short distances and then repeat her act. When the mother grouse figures that she has led the hungry animal far enough from her chicks she flies off, making a large circle before slipping back unseen to her young.

The female also uses this ruse on man. I remember a superb performance by one grouse mother. Our family farm was on a flattened ridge whose north boundary falls away, in some places almost clifflike, to the Delaware River below. I was walking along our back lane, which followed the ridge top, and was almost to where the lane opened out into a field when, coming around a sharp bend, I startled a grouse and her chicks. Leaves, chicks, and mother all scattered in wild confusion.

The female flew about fifty feet and upon landing went through her injured-wing routine. Having been decoyed before, I knew it was a ruse, but to see it again I followed her a short distance. After I had gone about two hundred feet I decided to go back to see the chicks, so I returned to where I had flushed the hen. I did not want to step on the chicks, so I got down on my hands and knees and cautiously explored each piece of the area before I crawled farther. The hen meanwhile flew back, came to within twenty-five feet of me, and again feigned an injured wing. Intent upon locating the chicks, I did not follow her. Not one to be ignored, the hen lay on her back and beat a tattoo against the ground with her wings as if she were in the throes of death. It was a convincing performance and one that would have lured any predator to her at once.

I alternated between looking for the chicks and watching the hen, which continued to tumble about and beat the leaves, while uttering short, high-pitched squeals. At length I found one chick huddled beneath a curled oak leaf. When I lifted the leaf from its back the

*Two-week-old ruffed grouse are old enough to fly a little.*

chick remained motionless. I examined the chick without touching it, replaced the leaf, and left the area.

In 1829, Alexander Wilson, an ornithologist, recorded an extraordinary experience with ruffed grouse. He discovered a female with only one chick. Upon sighting Wilson, the bird feigned a broken wing and tried to lure him away from her baby. When that failed, the mother grouse returned to the chick and, grasping it firmly in her bill, flew off to safety.

Another ornithologist had an unusual experience with grouse near Scotch Plains, New Jersey. He flushed a family of grouse and, as usual, the female attempted to lead him off by dragging her wing. He was surprised, however, when the male grouse suddenly appeared and joined the female in her attempt to decoy him by also feigning a broken wing. This action was unusual because the male grouse seldom helps the female in raising the family.

If the mother has been successful in leading danger away from her young, she sneaks back to reassemble them. When the chicks hear her *pe-ee-e-e-u-u-rr* sound they creep forth from their hiding places and she shepherds them out of the area as fast as they can travel.

The broken-wing trick is instinctive to the ruffed grouse, yet it is only used for about two weeks after the chicks hatch. Grouse chicks are extremely active for periods of about ten minutes, but a short rest seems to revitalize them. At four days they can jump about ten inches; in seven days they can fly to a perch twelve inches above the ground. When the chicks are eight days old, the fourth row of wing feathers has developed and the birds can fly horizontally from four to eight feet. After this, flight progress is rapid. As soon as the young can do so, both they and their mother roost in trees for the night. At this time the mother grouse gives up her broken-wing trick; it is no longer needed, since the chicks can now escape from all danger, except airborne predators, by flying.

Like every living thing, the ruffed grouse is subject to disease and

*The louse fly* (Lynchia americana) *is a parasite on ruffed grouse.*

parasitism. But there is no widespread evidence to indicate that either factor limits or controls population of the ruffed grouse, except under localized conditions.

External parasites such as ticks, fleas, lice, flies, and mites are usually easiest to see and so are most frequently noticed. Ticks (of the genus *Haemaphysalis*) are commonly found on the grouse and are sometimes numerous. In some areas of the north-central states, as many as 10 percent of the grouse may be infected by ticks. Robert G. Greene, in his studies of parasites on Minnesota grouse, found that the average bird had 640 ticks in September and 180 in October. Two grouse had records of 2,985 and 2,468 respectively. Ticks tend to concentrate on the grouse's head and neck. In addition to causing discomfort, large numbers of ticks can drain a considerable amount of blood and so weaken the host. Ticks are also notorious carriers of tularemia, a disease of rabbits, rodents, and other creatures.

Ticks hit their peak numbers in late summer. Their incidence is low in spring, builds up in the summer, and crashes after cold weather kills the adults. The eggs of the next generation pass the winter buried in the earth.

Louse, or hippoboscid, flies (*Lynchia americana*), that infest many wild birds, are also found on grouse. Numbers of these insects could be collected from grouse if the birds were placed in plastic bags the moment they were shot. I have seen louse flies fly off grouse as soon as an examination of the bird was made.*

Both lice and fleas are a rarity on grouse. Mites may be found in comparatively large numbers but are of no importance.

To gain relief from ectoparasites, the ruffed grouse will take frequent dust baths, usually in a depression in a bare area about twelve inches in diameter in an old roadway, under a rocky shelf, in a small clear spot in the forest, or along the edge of a clearing. I have seen grouse dust-bathe in the ashes left by a forest fire and have found two dusting places in dirt that was raised four feet or more above ground level by the roots of fallen trees. Occasionally grouse will dust-bathe in the punky dust of rotted wood.

On one of the regular canoe trips I conduct, taking boys to Canada, I was driving the leading vehicle on a dirt road going back to Lac Landron, our base camp. As I rounded a bend, I noticed a family of grouse dusting beneath a cutbank created by construction of the road. The summer had been dry, and the dirt and sand were like talcum powder. As we drew opposite the grouse, we stopped, jumped out, and ran over to corner them. The bank had a large overhang, forming a cul-de-sac. This was wilderness area (the road had just been built), and the ruffed grouse were exceedingly tame. They were

---

* The North American bloodsucking bird fly, *Lynchia americana,* has a wide range of hosts in three orders of birds—Falconiformes (vultures, kites, hawks, eagles, and falcons), Strigiformes (the owls), and Galliformes (grouse, pheasants, wild turkeys, etc.). The ruffed grouse serves as an important overwintering host for *Lynchia americana.* Of 147 juvenile ruffed grouse examined in New York State from June to August in 1935 and 1936, about 22 percent had from one up to a dozen of these bird flies in the plumage. Infestations of this fly on birds are usually light.—*The Editor.*

not alarmed by our truck, and by the time they became aware that we were a "danger" we were on top of them.

They naturally attempted to fly away but were blocked by the earthen wall. Before they could turn about, we were in front of the opening and caught two grouse with our hands while the rest thundered away. The boys all piled out of the truck to examine the birds. Some of them had never seen a grouse before. After everyone's curiosity was satisfied, we gave the grouse their freedom.

Dusting depressions are usually an inch or more deep, and there are often a few feathers or pieces of down in evidence. Grouse will scratch the dirt or dust loose with their feet and then lie on their sides

*A ruffed grouse dust bath on an anthill.*

and throw the loosened powder over their bodies with their wings and feet. The feathers of the bird's body are loosely held open so that the dust can penetrate to the skin, where it clogs the breathing holes of the parasites. When this happens some of the parasites may loosen their biting hold and drop off or be thrown off when the bird arises and shakes itself vigorously.

While dust baths may give an individual bird relief, they may not be a boon to all birds. Subsequent users of the same spot may pick up ticks that were on previous bathers. Both cottontail rabbits and hares also frequent dust baths used by grouse. In this manner there may be an interspecific exchange of parasites, particularly ticks. The chances are better than even that this is how grouse pick up ticks carrying tularemia.

Twenty-nine species of internal parasites are known to plague the ruffed grouse. Of the roundworms, *Dispharynx spiralis* and *Ascaridia bonasae,* although localized, are of the greatest importance. *Dispharynx* is a stomach worm which attacks the proventriculus not only of grouse but also of chickens, turkeys, guinea fowl, doves, and robins. It is a small whitish worm about ½ inch long that penetrates the gastric glands and can cause peritonitis. Although most grouse have less than a dozen of these worms, there is one record of 228 found in a single bird. Any grouse having more than 30 is usually doomed. They are most commonly found in grouse of New York, New Jersey, and the southern New England states.

The intestinal worm *Ascaridia* grows to a length of up to 4 inches and infests the alimentary tract, usually the small intestine. This worm takes its nutrition directly from the food being processed by the grouse. Large numbers of the worm deprive the grouse of needed food, and it may become emaciated or even die of starvation. Ontario, Canada, is the center of this parasite's range, with surrounding areas having a lesser occurrence.

Seven species of tapeworms have been reported in ruffed grouse, most in the small intestine. Some of the species are microscopic and thus they are commonly overlooked. Except in rare cases they seem to have no adverse effect on the health of the grouse.

Of the nine species of protozoa known to infect grouse, only two are of importance. Coccidiosis, a disease common to domestic fowl, is also common among pen-reared grouse but is not often found in birds in the wild. Coccidia usually develop in the walls of the small intestine and, where present in large numbers, cause a disruption in the bird's digestive processes.

A blood parasite, *Leucocytozoon bonasae*, causes a malarialike disease in ruffed grouse, so far known only in grouse in Ontario, Minnesota, and Michigan. Because it can become epizootic, its incidence is carefully watched.

Any or most of these parasites and diseases may be fatal to the ruffed grouse, but fortunately none has ever been experienced on a truly large scale. While many of these factors may contribute to the decline of the grouse, there is no concrete evidence that any were the decisive factor. As the numbers of the ruffed grouse increase cyclically, the incidence of disease and parasitism also increases, but this is to be expected, because the greater the exposure between grouse, the greater the chance each has of contracting diseases and parasites.

As the summer advances, most of the male ruffed grouse have ceased their drumming, and some join with the female and her young. It is a time of somnolence. Food is plentiful and easily secured, which leaves time for grouse to take dust baths and skulk in the shade.

When the temperature is high, the grouse will cool itself by rapid inhalation and exhalation of breath. This causes a heat exchange by vaporization of the heated body fluids in the lungs and air sacs. To maintain its body requirements, the grouse will have to drink more water.

After about eight weeks the young grouse have lost most of their

*Three-week-old ruffed grouse. By now the chicks can fly quite far and rise quite high in the air.*

down and are clothed in their juvenile plumage. The last of the down is fast worn off the tips of these feathers. Sex can be told at this time by the development of color in the male's eye patch and some of the young males may strut once in a while. Females may proclaim their sex by becoming more vociferous.

Toward the end of July, grouse tend to become secretive because the adults are going into their annual molt. These birds have been losing body feathers sporadically since early spring, to be cooler during the hot weather. Now, however, all or most of the primary wing feathers are lost at one time, and for a short period the grouse may be flightless. Handicapped by such a condition, the birds do everything possible to avoid attracting attention.

While the adult grouse are getting their new feathers, the chicks are gaining their adult feathers. One can see the difference between the young and the adults by examining the first- and second-wing primary feathers. Although the young grouse sheds the other eight juvenile primary feathers now, it retains the first two until the following summer. These two juvenile feathers have pointed tips, while the tips of the same two feathers on an adult bird are rounded. Thus, with the bird in the hand, it is comparatively easy to tell whether it is younger or older than one year.

While the ruffed grouse goes on about its business of living, so do all other types of wildlife, including the grouse's predators. Through diseases, accidents, weather, and predation, the grouse ranks are thinned so that by the end of summer the average brood has been reduced from eleven to seven juveniles.

*The worn, rounded tips of the primary feathers show this to be the wing of an adult bird.*

# Autumn

I<small>T CAN'T REALLY BE SAID</small> that autumn is a quiet period, because for some creatures it is the time of peak activity. Yet it is the one time of the year when nature seems content to rest. The weather is the finest of the year, each day outdoing the last. The nights are cool but the days are still warm, and the sunlit hours are brisk, bright, invigorating.

Autumn brings about an increased tempo in the lives of the ruffed grouse, for September is dispersal time. (This period has also been called the "crazy season" or the "fall shuffle.") Much has been said and written about this phenomenon, but it is only recently that comprehensive studies have been made.

During the last part of August and the first week of September the broods break up. At first, grouse families are still together in their home range, usually a quarter to a half mile across, but each grouse seems to be pushing restlessly against the invisible boundaries defining that range. There may also be a temporary intermingling of family groups, because of overlapping ranges. This restlessness continues for two to three weeks, and then the birds disperse.

During dispersal, ruffed grouse are famous for flying into windows. Although grouse and other birds fly into windows during every month of the year, this activity peaks in October. Smaller birds usually crash into windows during migration, with a larger toll being taken during the autumn than in the spring. Sporting magazines, conservation magazines, and many newspapers report these incidents, starting in

September and culminating in November. It is odd that a grouse capable of flying through dense cover, twisting and turning its body and seldom touching a branch, will run smack into the window of a house.

Many theories have been put forth to explain these incidents. One is that these grouse are intoxicated, and this does happen to many wild animals. The berries and fruits of certain plants have a high sugar content, and when the dead-ripe fruits fall and lie in the sun, the juices become fermented. I have often seen bees and yellow jackets so drunk they couldn't fly. Robins, cedar waxwings, and cardinals feeding on the fermented berries of Tatarian honeysuckle have gotten into the same condition. So it is easy to see that ruffed grouse could become inebriated, but I don't think this is the explanation.

Another theory is that young grouse—and it is mainly the young that crash into windows—are flying about in a panic caused by falling leaves. More grouse are killed by airborne predators than from all other types combined. Grouse are constantly alert to the slightest movement in their area, particularly movement in the air. As the leaves start to fall, it must be a traumatic experience to young grouse that have never seen this occurrence before. Falling leaves may prompt panic in some of the grouse, but I don't think this is the answer, either.

One October a ruffed grouse crashed through a storm window in my kitchen. The bird was killed and hung between the broken storm sash and the unbroken inner window. This was the second grouse that had flown into a window of my home. Neither had greenery in them, so the grouse could not have mistaken the windows for more forest cover.*

---

* Grouse also fly into the sides of buildings and into fences during the fall shuffle. There is a theory that birds fly into window glass because they see the trees and shrubs reflected there as an extension of the yard or garden. Flying into a reflected environment may be the reason that so many birds are stunned, crippled, or killed by striking picture windows each year. It is significant that when awnings are lowered over part of the window, eliminating or at least partly covering the reflected image, losses of birds from striking the glass decrease markedly.—*The Editor.*

*Autumn*

The development of radiotelemetry devices has given us new insights into the behavior patterns of ruffed grouse during the brood breakup and dispersal periods. Geoffrey A. Godfrey and William H. Marshall in 1964 attached radios to some grouse in the Cloquet Forest Preserve in Minnesota and monitored the birds' daily activities. Their findings on the dispersal of ruffed grouse are analogous to the findings of the Craighead brothers on the denning of grizzly bears. In both instances, the activities of both species were controlled by photo-

*The ruffed grouse that crashed through my kitchen window.*

periodism and triggered by approaching storm fronts.

Godfrey and Marshall found that the breakup period began about September 7. Seventeen days later, on September 24, as the temperature dropped and rain started to fall, three of the grouse, within a period of hours, started to disperse. Their movements were not meandering but an almost beeline egress. Although the grouse headed in different directions, their travels were in as straight a line as it was possible for them to move in, to take advantage of existing cover. On October 7, the same climatic conditions set two more grouse in motion.

The birds traveled an average of four days during dispersal, with all movement being confined to the daylight hours. They moved through different types of habitat for a daily average distance of a minimum 2,071 feet to a maximum 3,992 feet. One grouse traveled 5,709 feet in one day. While one bird moved only .90 of a mile, another moved 3.02 miles from its former home range. While the birds in this study group were undoubtedly invading habitats frequented by other grouse, the places they had vacated were being filled by grouse dispersing from still different areas. This so-called "shuffle" is of tremendous importance to the grouse because it ensures a constant influx of new breeding stock into each area and precludes the possibility of interbreeding. This pattern of dispersal and the setting up of new territories closely parallels that of the red grouse of Scotland.

Investigations carried out in various states by different people have proved what was generally known—that it is the immature birds that do most of the moving and that the adult birds are usually sedentary. Among both adults and juveniles, it was found that females travel the farthest. Most of the grouse traveled between 1.5 and 3 miles, while a few traveled 10 to 19 miles. James B. Hale and Robert S. Dorney, in their grouse-dispersal studies in Wisconsin, have recorded the greatest distance I can find for the ruffed grouse. A female grouse

*Ruffed grouse usually disperse on foot.*

they had banded on September 25, 1956, was shot on November 10, 1957, 71 miles away.

A ruffed grouse that is flying, like a deer that is running, is at a distinct disadvantage. It is true that each method of locomotion rapidly puts distance between the creature and whatever scared it in the first place, but the animal is also prevented from observing whatever may be dangerous in the area it is entering. Any potential prey animal in rapid motion is always noticed by all predators much more quickly than one which moves stealthily or slowly. Both grouse and deer skulk about whenever possible, and grouse in dispersal usually walk from place to place.

During the Minnesota studies, one of the grouse that was being followed by radio made two flights. What prompted the grouse to fly? The researchers don't know.

In addition to crashing through windows, the ruffed grouse sometimes collides with natural obstacles. Edward Howe Forbush reported on a grouse that had flown into a forked stick. The collision was fatal because the grouse impaled its breast upon one prong of the stick while the other tore the bird's head and neck from the body. While most of these collisions are probably fatal, John K. Terres reported a grouse picked up by Dr. Arthur A. Allen in his studies that had a fair-sized twig forced down its throat while flying. The bird survived, and the twig eventually was covered by membranous tissue.

The territory that young birds select in fall must have sufficient food and cover. When the territory has been selected, the grouse spend a great deal of time exploring the area. This exploration is important to survival: the better the grouse knows its area, the better its chances of escaping from enemies. For male grouse the areas chosen will probably be their home territory for the rest of their lives. Some of the males, both migrant young ones and resident adults, may now do some drumming to proclaim their territorial rights.

Grouse research material bears out my observations that, generally, the ruffed grouse are now leading solitary lives. However, for reasons not yet known, some grouse behave otherwise in fall and are social. As many hunters know, coveys of grouse are often flushed during the hunting season, and I have myself flushed as many as eight birds in one covey in November. Are these concentrations a reassembling of grouse or are they groups that just did not split up? I tend to believe it is the former condition, although I cannot prove it. The New York State study (Bump *et al.*) records that during dispersal time all of their penned birds became increasingly nervous and wild. They were responding to the same stimuli as the wild grouse but because of the pens they were unable to move out. The same study also suggests that coveys of grouse seen in the winter result from birds congregating in areas offering the maximum shelter from storms. I can agree, but I can find no explanation for the coveys that are together in November when storm shelter has not yet become important.

Shortage of food is not a factor because, except in rare instances, autumn provides a glut of food. At this time of the year the grouse's diet is about 98 percent vegetable matter. The dogwoods, both gray and flowering, produce large quantities of berries, as do the serviceberry, barberry, viburnums, and cranberry. In northern areas bunchberry is an important food crop. Wherever they are found, wild grapes are avidly eaten. Mast crops such as beechnuts are sporadic, although acorns are a reliable food source. (It is amazing that grouse are capable of swallowing some of the larger acorns.) Thorn apples, or hawthorn and cultivated apples, make up a large part of the grouse's diet at this time. Although grouse will eat the fruit, they are primarily interested in appleseeds and prefer red apples to yellow ones. When they are feeding in orchards where both red and yellow apples are growing, they will eat the red ones first. On such lush fare the adults soon reach their heaviest weights of the year, the males averaging 23.3 ounces and females 20.9 ounces.

*Grouse love wild grapes and will also eat beechnuts.*

*The toe scales that grow each fall on the ruffed grouse's foot act as snowshoes.*

Grouse are primarily northern birds, and nature provides special adaptations for their toes which enable them to walk on the top of the snow. They are in effect fitted with snowshoes, for in October the grouse develop cuticular outgrowths along the outside edges of each toe called pectinations. These comblike appendages, or scales, measure 2 to 3 millimeters, about $\frac{1}{10}$ inch, or one half the width of the toe itself. The growth is along both sides of each toe, so the toe surface is effectively doubled. These "snowshoes" allow the grouse to walk on the top of all but the very softest snow without sinking in. The ruffed grouse's far-northern cousins, the ptarmigans, have similar feathers on their toes that serve the same purpose. One big difference is that the grouse loses its toe scales in the spring while the ptarmigan retains feathers on its feet year round.

A young grouse is considered to be full-grown by September 1. Both the young and the adults will be in full plumage at this time, having a full complement of feathers. In addition to having primary feathers with rounded tips, in contrast to the sharp-pointed tips on the young birds' first and second primary feathers, the adults can also be told because all of their primary feathers will have blood in the shaft until the end of the year. Also, the web of skin on the wing of a young bird is much thinner than is that of the adult. The determination of age by these techniques is of interest chiefly to game managers and wildlife researchers. Most hunters are only interested in finding the grouse. They usually check to see if a bird is male or female, but few go beyond that. However, it is important that the hunter be aware of what game managers are trying to do, because checking the age composition of the birds taken reveals whether the breeding season has been a success or not. Game managers know that much of their research is dependent on the hunters' cooperation, because hunters handle far more grouse than game managers have access to.

Ruffed grouse hunters are the elite among the bird-shooting fraternity. By this I mean only that ruffed grouse hunters have to hunt harder, walk farther (through the most dense cover on the most difficult terrain), fire more shots, and expect poorer results than other bird hunters. These trials make them a breed apart; it not only toughens their muscles but their spiritual fibers as well. The grouse hunter knows before he starts out that he will not come back laden with game. He knows that he is seeking an elusive quarry, but he also knows that in seeking this bird he will be afield at the finest time of the year. The grouse is a noble bird, and I feel that hunting it enriches the hunter.

The main area of disagreement for grouse hunters is between those who hunt with a dog and those who do not. There is much to be said for both methods. More hunters go out without a dog, but perhaps this is because good grouse dogs are rare. I have hunted both ways and have perhaps gotten more pleasure—but not more game—out of working with a dog.

No matter which way you hunt, the more knowledge you have about the ruffed grouse, the higher your chances of success are bound to be. Dedicated grouse hunters go out in the spring to locate the males on their drumming logs. Each site that they can locate in the spring will be a focal point for at least one male and perhaps more in the fall.

*The English setter is a good grouse dog.*

By the time that most states have opened their hunting season, the grouse have abandoned the openings and clearings they have frequented during the summer and have sought cover in thicker brush or moved to the uplands. Most of the broods have scattered.

A smart hunter will open the crop of the first grouse he bags to see what the bird has been feeding on and will then hunt such locations. Some years, however, there is such an abundance of grouse food that checking the crop doesn't help; the grouse may be feeding on almost everything. (Then, too, a lot of hunters don't recognize the food particles even when they see them.)

An experienced hunter will find the largest number of grouse because he will hunt the spots where he previously flushed them. So long as the habitat remains the same, the grouse will continue to frequent such spots. Grouse are punctual; if they are feeding in a given area at a certain time today, they will probably be feeding in the same spot at the same time tomorrow. So if the food, cover, and cycle are right, the grouse will be in the same area year after year.

At the beginning of the hunting season the majority of the birds shot are young grouse, because the ratio of young grouse to adults is higher and the young are inexperienced. Grouse soon become wary, and if a young grouse escapes the first fusillade of shots its chances of survival are increased tremendously.

The thundering sound of a flying grouse's wings is made by a *startled* grouse. It is heard more frequently in the early part of the season than later on. As the grouse are hunted and become more wary, they begin to flush at greater distances. When a grouse that has been "educated" sees a hunter approaching, it will often slip behind a tree and flush from behind cover. Grouse, when starting to fly, usually take three or four short running steps before they are airborne. If the day is calm the grouse will take off in the direction of the heaviest cover. On a windy day the grouse, as do all birds, takes off into the wind.

*Multiflora rose and pine provide food and shelter. The grouse usually feed here at 4 P.M. each day in fall and winter.*

A hunter knowing these facts can use them by hunting with a light wind behind him so that the grouse will flush toward him. Sometimes the grouse will hold tight, allowing the hunter to walk past so it can flush out behind and still take advantage of the breeze. Extremely windy days are usually poor for hunting of any kind. The action of the wind-tossed branches makes all wildlife high-strung and nervous, and the grouse will flush wildly.

Grouse that are flushed on a hill have a tendency to fly up the side. They may drop at first, but almost invariably they curve and glide back up. Most grouse are hunted in heavy cover and the birds, when flushed, fly toward the heaviest cover in the area. Sometimes, though, the cover is so dense that it is difficult for even a grouse to wend its way through, and at such times the bird will ascend steeply or "tower" to get in the clear. Old-time grouse hunters claim that, in regular cover, the female grouse seldom rises higher than ten to fifteen feet above the ground as she flies and that the higher-flying birds are the males. Checking the sex of birds which have been shot under such conditions seems to bear out this observation.

*105*

The favored guns for grouse hunting are the light 16- and 20-gauge side-by-side double-barreled shotguns weighing between 6 and 7 pounds. Because most of the shooting is done at ranges of twenty to thirty yards or even closer, an open boring of either cylinder and improved cylinder, or improved cylinder and modified in the right and left barrels, are good combinations. Either No. 7½ or 8 shot will give a good uniform pattern, and these are the sizes most commonly used.

I am fully aware that the foregoing paragraph will probably bring howls of anguish from multitudes of grouse hunters. You can no more select a gun for a man than you could select a wife for him. Some hunters swear that the over-and-under shotgun is the best for grouse; others prefer a double-barrel, a pump or an automatic. Still others want modified cylinders for close shots and a full choke to reach out for the long shots. Some will want No. 9 shot for close shots; others will want No. 6 for better brush penetration. I am not attempting to tell anyone what to use; I am merely describing what the majority of grouse hunters have found to be best over the years.

A man carrying a gun weighing 6 pounds will be much more able to shoot after several hours of hunting than will the hunter carrying a heavier gun. The 26-inch barrels are just a little easier to swing in heavy brush and to get into action on a rapidly disappearing target. And as a ruffed grouse is not a particularly hard bird to drop, the 7½ and 8 shot sizes make a most dense pattern. However, the real criteria in choosing any gun should be that it fits you, that you are thoroughly familiar with it, that it delivers a good pattern using the shells you have selected, and that it allows you to kill grouse without crippling them.

The key to attaining proficiency with any gun is to use it, and to use it as often as possible. Grouse hunting is always an off-balance, unprepared type of shooting, and only practice leads to proficiency. Remember, almost any grouse seen in regular cover is within the average shotgun range; shoot. Among even the most expert hunters an average of two grouse for every five shots is considered excellent.

Grouse hunters who do not use a dog have found that they can have good luck if they walk slowly through good grouse habitat, pausing now and then to scan the area ahead of them. By so doing, they make less noise to attract the grouse's attention and also have a good chance to see the grouse moving before it sees them. A grouse will not run ahead of the hunter like a pheasant, but it will attempt to get into heavy cover. If a grouse has been sighted going into such cover, the hunter usually makes quite a bit of noise advancing on the spot and then stands absolutely still. The grouse knows where the hunter is by the noise he makes but will become puzzled when the noise stops. In the ensuing war of nerves, the grouse usually breaks first and

*A ruffed grouse sneaking through heavy cover.*

whirrs up out of the cover to seek sanctuary elsewhere. The alert hunter will have noted all possible flight channels and knows that where the cover is heaviest is the spot the grouse will try to reach. Even if the grouse succeeds in flying out behind protective cover, many hunters will shoot even if they don't aim at the grouse; they know that a grouse that is shot at will usually fly a shorter distance than one that is not. The hunter will mark the bird's flight line and will probably be able to flush the bird again and perhaps get a shot at it.

A hunter who shoots in a grouse's direction should spare no effort in trying to find what may be a downed bird. A wounded bird will be desperate to conceal itself. Even a bird that is killed while in the air may be very hard to find, so well do its colors and patterning blend in with the leaves of the forest floor. A good dog proves invaluable in retrieving downed birds.

Setters and, to a lesser extent, Brittany spaniels and some pointers, are the dogs most commonly used for hunting grouse because they locate the birds but try not to flush them. A dog that is good on grouse is never used to hunt pheasants, because most pheasants will not hold still. When this happens most dogs will break the point they have been holding and follow the pheasant. Eventually the dog will refuse to hold a point and, when used on grouse, will flush the birds far out of the hunter's range.

Many hunters who do not have time to train their dogs themselves will ship them off to a trainer who specializes in such work. Many of these trainers live in Canada, where they have an almost unlimited supply of grouse to work on. The main drawback to this system is that a dog trained on unwary wilderness grouse still has a lot to learn before it can begin to cope with the wildly flushing grouse of our more settled areas.

Although the ruffed grouse holds much better for a dog than a pheasant does, it will usually work its way through the thicket that the dog is pointing at. The hunter has to be prepared either to go around

*A good dog is invaluable for retrieving ruffed grouse.*

the thicket to flush the bird or to shoot over the top if the brush is low enough to permit it. A bold approach to a pointing dog is the best procedure, as the grouse already knows just where the danger is located.

Some grouse when flushed will seek sanctuary in the tops of tall hemlocks. Perching high in the tree, the birds are not likely to be seen by hunters and cannot be located by dogs.

Henry Zeman of Grand Rapids, Michigan, is an unusual hunter who shoots at grouse with a gun and a camera at the same time. Zeman is a newspaper photographer who has mounted an automatic 35-mm camera on a special brace that rides on his back. By using a wide-angle lens, the hunter can cover both himself and his quarry. When a grouse is flushed, Zeman triggers both the camera and his gun. He has gotten some excellent photographs by this method, but he certainly wipes out most of the excuses for missing that other hunters use. In Zeman's case all of the action has been recorded on film.

Predation of the ruffed grouse is probably lightest during the autumn. At this season all grouse can fly, and they regularly roost in the trees at night, effectively foiling the foxes. As the leaves are still on some of the trees, even aerial predators have some trouble finding them. The lack of snow means that the activities of such buffer species as mice and rats can still be seen, and so they take the pressure off the grouse. Man is commonly thought to be the ruffed grouse's greatest enemy. To my mind this means man the builder, not man the hunter.

It has been figured that the ruffed grouse population as a whole declines about 50 percent during the month and a half to two months that a hunting season is allowed in most states. But the New York State study showed that in general hunters take only 15 percent of a year-round total grouse population.

Studies carried out in Michigan by Walter L. Palmer and Carl L. Bennett, Jr., seem conclusive. From 1950 through 1962, two identical kinds of habitat areas were studied. One was a refuge where no hunt-

*The author with male and female ruffed grouse, springer spaniel, and Browning automatic .20-gauge gun.*

ing was allowed; the other an open hunting area where the pressure was great. The populations of the grouse fluctuated from year to year, but they stayed correspondingly the same in both areas. The decrease during the autumn hunting period was the same in the unhunted area as it was where hunting was allowed. The decline over the winter was slightly greater on the unhunted area than on the hunted tract (no reason was established for this but it was definitely not due to hunting), but in the summer the increase in the number of grouse was slightly higher on the unhunted tract, which compensated for the greater decrease during the winter. September of each year found both populations almost identical. Hunters took 30 percent of the estimated grouse population each year, and it was believed that the grouse population could have easily withstood a 50-percent take. The hunters took 75 percent of their birds in the first fifteen days of the grouse-hunting season and 95 percent of their total take in the first thirty days. The researchers' conclusions were that the seasons could be opened early or kept open later without doing any harm to the annual grouse population.

My own state of New Jersey has lengthened the grouse-hunting season from five weeks to twelve weeks; the longer season allows the hunters more days afield but has done nothing to alter our grouse population. (There are few if any hunters who take advantage of that many extra days.)

It all boils down to the fact that when the grouse population is high, hunters hunt them; when the numbers of grouse drop, so do the numbers of hunters.

To see if a grouse population could be shot off, New York State hired two professional hunters in the mid 1930s to try to do just that. The experiment was carried out for three years on three different plots of land of one square mile each. The hunters, hunting every chance they had, got to know not only each covert but each grouse, and they still could not shoot them out. As the grouse population dropped, the remaining birds became so wary that they continually flushed far out of gun range.

As autumn fades, the grouse population has been reduced to about 25 percent of the peak in June.

*I always flush grouse at this fencerow but almost never get a shot.*

*Winter is a bleak season.*

# Winter

WINTER IS A TIME of testing. For many animals, it is the most difficult time of the year. Food and cover are in short supply. Among wildlife, those that survive are the strongest, or the fastest, or the most intelligent, or the most adaptable, or the most responsive to stimuli; they are the breeding stock for the next generation. Each wild creature in the world today epitomizes natural selection; it is the result of nature's pressures and the shaping of each animal and the adaptive response of each to its role and place in the environment.

In the warm seasons there is often a surfeit of food and, with most species, a plentitude of creatures to utilize it. An ecological pyramid is built based on the green growing things, tapering to the creatures which feed on vegetation, and capped by the predators. As the season of productivity is shut down with the advent of cold weather, the pressure applied by one species upon another becomes more relentless. Such pressure is augmented by falling temperatures, increased wind velocity, and the accumulations of ice or snow.

The start of winter is not a calendar event but is marked by heavy, killing frosts. Contrary to popular conceptions, the bright colors of autumn are in evidence before the heavy frosts come. The frosts hasten the fall of the leaves. Suddenly, one is aware that it is now possible to see hundreds of yards into forests that had previously been screened. The frosts also kill the herbaceous plants—the weeds, herbs, and tops of the grasses—causing all but the most stiff-spined stalks to fall, and those stalks will later be flattened by ice storms and the weight of the snow. Thus the fields become devoid of cover.

Animals that migrate have done so. Animals that hibernate have done so. Animals that remain to face the onslaught of winter soon find that their range is dictated by the weather, which soon forces them to seek out the remaining shelter—brushy hedgerows, thickets, hollows, gullies, or swamps. The seeking out of such sheltered spots causes a concentration of wildlife, with a resultant competition for cover and food not only between individuals but between species as well.

Over a large part of the ruffed grouse's range, the white-tailed deer and the varying hare are two of its main competitors. This competition is keener over cover than over food. Much of our mature woodlands, without an understory of saplings and shrubs, provide little in the way of either food or cover for most wildlife.

Ruffed grouse winter range will almost always be in areas where there is at least a scattering of evergreen trees, which the grouse

*White-tailed buck in winter.*

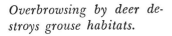

*The snowshoe hare competes for cover with the grouse.*

favor for roosting. The conifers, where the lower branches have not been browsed by deer, make good shelter—shelter that is tepeelike when heavy snows bend those branches to earth. The evergreens provide protection from cold and storms during periods of high wind, and their screening branches prevent the grouse from being silhouetted as they are when they perch on the bare limbs of deciduous trees —where they must depend on immobility for protection (or flight). The grouse instinctively know that they are easily seen moving against a white expanse of snow. I have seen alarmed grouse "freeze" and hold their position for at least a half hour.

Grouse habitat management has always stressed the importance of evergreens. So it came as a surprise when Gullion and Marshall proved that on the Cloquet Forest Research Center in Minnesota

*Overbrowsing by deer destroys grouse habitats.*

*A ruffed grouse in winter is silhouetted against the snow.*

a ruffed grouse's chance of survival was better in "bean-pole" woods than in areas that had evergreen trees. (A bean-pole woods is a heavy growth of young trees—fifteen to twenty years old—that are competing for sunlight. They will be thin, straight, and tall, with few or no branches except at their leafy tops and almost no undergrowth on the shady ground beneath them.)

Gullion and Marshall's conclusions were based on the fact that hawks, such as the Cooper's and the goshawk, and owls, such as the great horned and barred, all frequent evergreen trees for the protection they afford. From such vantage points these predators can drop down on the grouse.*

* In recognition of the valuable ecological role of predatory birds in their relation to other animals in the environment, most states legally protect most hawks and owls from killing or possession; eagles are protected by both federal and state laws. In March, 1972, the governments of the United States and Mexico, through an amendment to the Migratory Bird Treaty Act of 1936, gave immediate protection to all birds of prey in both countries. These include falcons, caracaras, eagles, hawks, kites, ospreys, owls, vultures, and the California condor.—*The Editor.*

Nevertheless, in my observation, ruffed grouse prefer an area with some evergreen trees despite the risks. During the month of January, 1970, four ruffed grouse were roosting nightly in a clump of forty-feet-high Norway spruces at the edge of my driveway and only about fifty feet from a main macadam road. In a radius of within perhaps six hundred feet of the spruces, there are five houses; at three of these houses there are cats and at four there are dogs. In spite of these obstacles, the grouse preferred to sleep in my few evergreens rather than stay in the many acres of bean-pole woods in and around my property.

Snow is another survival factor. In the winter when the ground is bare, grouse roost in trees. When the snow has a crust on it, grouse also roost in trees. When there are three to six inches of soft snow on

*A ruffed grouse in soft snow, kept from sinking by his "snowshoes."*

the ground, the grouse may roost in trees or they may roost on the snow, settling their bodies into a shallow hole. When there are ten to twelve inches or more of dry soft snow, many grouse prefer to roost beneath the snow.

The snow in my area is often heavy and wet, and grouse seldom roost beneath it because of its tendency to freeze. Farther north, the colder weather produces a drier, fluffier snow, so more ruffed grouse use it as a blanket. The insulating quality of soft snow is so great that the temperature may be as much as 50 degrees higher for the grouse buried beneath the snow's surface than for one exposed to the elements above the snow.

The coldest part of each twenty-four-hour period is from 11 P.M. till dawn. The thermometer seldom drops much after 11 P.M., because the inversion of temperature is usually complete about that time. Most animals while sleeping undergo a lowering of their metabolic processes, with a resultant drop in body temperature. For animals that are diurnal, the drop in atmospheric temperature coincides with the drop in body temperature. While sleeping during normal summer conditions, the bird's temperature drops as much as 2 degrees. However, in tests, birds that became wet or were exposed to increased wind velocity or extreme cold weather experienced a drop in body temperature of as much as 11 degrees. Proper snow conditions are essential for ruffed grouse to survive in the northern part of its range.

Studies show that, when snow conditions are right, grouse will venture farther out into clear patches of aspen to feed. If disturbed, they fly into the snow to hide. At such times snow takes the place of vegetative cover.

Tom Prawdzik, a biologist working for the Michigan Department of Conservation, photographed just such a happening. While he was on a trip to inspect the condition of deer yarding, a ruffed grouse suddenly plunged into the snow a few feet away. The bird was being chased by a Cooper's hawk. When the grouse hit the snow the hawk veered off, although the grouse was not yet completely hidden from sight; but it shuffled its body rapidly from side to side and, with this burrowing motion, soon disappeared beneath the snow.

Curious, Prawdzik lifted the grouse from its hiding place and set it on top of the snow. Again in just a few moments the grouse had burrowed its way down beneath the surface. Not having his camera with him, Prawdzik again recovered the grouse and carried it back to where he had parked his automobile. The bird's fear of the hawk was greater than its fear of man, and it made no attempt to escape by flying. Securing his camera, Prawdzik again placed the grouse on the snow and photographed its burrowing technique. Within moments the grouse had disappeared from view. This time the grouse was allowed to remain hidden in the snow. When Prawdzik came back the next morning to check on the deer and the grouse, he found that the grouse had spent the night there in safety and had flown out of

*Grouse tracks in the snow: two birds on foot, and wing marks made by takeoff.*

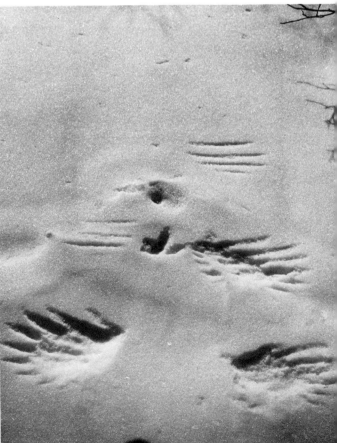

its hiding place in the snow sometime prior to his arrival.

Some grouse, in preparing for the night, walk into the snow and settle themselves, as their tracks plainly show. However, most grouse simply fold their wings and fly into the snow head first so that they don't leave any telltale tracks. The birds instinctively know that tracks leading to their submerged roosting spot are an open invitation to any of the four-footed predators that hunt by scent. Even so, the bird's breath may melt a little hole up through the snow through which its scent can escape.

Predators such as the fox can locate grouse even when buried. Most of the time the grouse escape, however. Even under the snow grouse are very alert, and the discovery of danger by one bird will cause others buried in the immediate vicinity to burst out of the snow, too.

On occasion, wildlife biologists have discovered grouse beneath the snow by their breathing holes. According to published reports, however, they don't have much better success at catching grouse beneath the snow than foxes do.

Sometimes after the grouse has plunged beneath the snow's surface, it will push its way forward, creating a short tunnel. Every once in a while it pops its head back out above the surface to watch for danger. When satisfied it has not been seen, it will then settle down for the night. Evidence in the form of tracks suggests that sometimes grouse will attempt to feed on plants beneath the snow. Tracks also prove that most of the grouse emerging from snow cover do so by flying out rather than by walking out. There are also records of grouse killing themselves by striking some object hidden beneath the snow that they flew into.

In addition to the rare circumstance in which a grouse is discovered and caught beneath the snow by a predator, it is equally rare for grouse to be trapped beneath the surface of the snow by a freezing rain. It will not burrow into snow that is thawing. Not only will such snow probably freeze, but, as the water content in the snow rises, the air content diminishes and so does its insulating quality.

A grouse trapped beneath the snow by a freezing rain is not necessarily lost. As the snow beneath is still dry, the grouse remains warm, and it can eat snow for moisture. Tests have proved that, in winter, a grouse must have access to snow or water every day if it is to survive. Some have stayed alive locked beneath snow for up to a week.

Many factors affect starvation in ruffed grouse: temperature, wind velocity, length of time without water or food, and the bird's general weight and body condition. A healthy adult grouse can go without food for ten days if it has access to water. Beyond ten days, or if the bird's body weight drops to less than 14 ounces, the grouse has little chance of survival, even if it is then supplied with unlimited food and water.

*Red fox hunting in snow.*

A grouse needs more grit in the winter because of the coarseness of the food it is ingesting. When the entire area is covered with snow, grouse will frequently be seen picking up grit along roadsides. Almost all country roads today are cleared of snow shortly after storms end. Often the roads are plowed deep enough to expose the bare earth and gravel at the edge of the road. Many country roads are macadamized, and their black surfaces absorb and reflect the sun, melting the snow to expose needed gravel. Many states use fine gravel instead of salt, or gravel mixed with salt, to provide traction on icy roads. The grouse will eat this material, too. Some of the hard seeds that grouse ingest in winter also perform a grinding function. Seeds of such plants as hawthorn, smilax, dogwood, sumac, and rose are harder than other foods and can serve as grit. In most grouse country, there are small spring-fed streams that remain unfrozen despite the coldest weather. The edges of such streams will be frequented by grouse because they provide almost everything a grouse needs: water, grit, and, even in winter, some types of greens growing in the warmer water that grouse can eat.

It is unusual for a freezing rain to come in midwinter, but when it does, it is the single most devastating factor a grouse must contend with. Because of the tremendous variety of foods that a grouse can and will eat, the birds almost never starve unless there is an ice storm. A rain that encases every tree, branch, and twig with ice is the key that effectively locks the grouse's food larder. This condition can exist as long as the weather remains cold and there is no wind. An extended period of icing results in hardship or, in extreme cases, even death.

If the wind comes up after an ice storm, the swaying of the branches will frequently crack the ice, causing some of it to drop off and expose the buds as food. An extremely heavy ice storm will strip the branches from the trees or break them down entirely, exposing food for grouse.

A severe ice storm, even one that kills some grouse may prove to

*Ice-coated birch catkins can mean disaster for the grouse.*

be a boon to the survivors. A really bad storm may kill or destroy thousands of trees, thus creating a hole in the forest's canopy. The increased sunlight reaching the forest floor will stimulate new plant growth, greatly increasing the food supply for future generations of grouse.

The same deep snow that provides protection for the grouse also provides shelter for rats, mice, voles, and lemmings. These small rodents welcome the snow because beneath its cover they can tunnel out networks of interlocking paths, free from fear of discovery. Deprived of these "buffer species," predators turn to ptarmigans, grouse, hares, and rabbits.

While the New York State study (Bump *et al.*) shows that the great horned owl, the goshawk, and the fox are responsible for the death of 20 percent of all grouse killed each year, it also proves that habitat and not predation is the limiting factor in the ruffed grouse population (or, for that matter, in any wildlife population).

A similar conclusion was reached by Paul Errington, who, while studying quail populations in the Prairie du Sac area of Wisconsin in the 1930s and 1940s, also observed the numerical relation between the ruffed grouse wintering in the area and the resident great horned owls. When the grouse population rose above twenty, owl predation increased; when the population dropped, so did the pressure from the predators. Again, if the environment is favorable for any species, predation is not a limiting factor.

In the wintertime a ruffed grouse's diet is 100 percent vegetable matter. Its favored food is the buds of the aspen tree, but it also eats the buds of the apple tree, hazelnut, blueberry, blackberry, raspberry, wild cherry, willow, dogwood, birch, beech, and maple. The leaves of everbearing plants such as mountain laurel, wintergreen, sheep sorrel, wood fern, Christmas fern, and rattlesnake fern are also taken.

*Dogwood, cedar, and birch trees make a fine habitat for grouse. I flushed one here as I walked in for the photo.*

I found a grouse killed on the road whose crop bulged with kernels it had gleaned from corn missed by the picker.

In places where they grow, then, the male aspen tree is the most important item to the grouse, providing both food and cover. Grouse feeding in aspen trees display a definite pattern. They enter the trees at the lower branches and work their way up to the top, usually in a spiral fashion. They seldom remain in one spot but pick off a few buds, then move upward and pick some more. The limb they vacate is never picked clean, as if the birds, like the grazing or browsing mam-

*Male aspen buds are an important winter food for grouse.*

mals, move on to "greener pastures" elsewhere. This movement is desirable because it prevents the birds from harming any individual tree. The grouse in feeding will, if possible, select a variety of foods. This also prevents excessive damage to one food species.

In checking grouse crops I usually find a preponderance of one food but have never found one food exclusively. The elasticity of a grouse's crop is a source of constant amazement to me. The food that the grouse is feeding upon in the wintertime has a low nutrient content, so that a vast amount of it must pass through the digestive system if the grouse is to survive.

The largest volume of food that I have measured from a ruffed grouse's crop was about 5 ounces, most of it seed from wild barberry bushes. A study made in the George Washington National Forest in West Virginia turned up a grouse crop that contained 118.5 cubic centimeters, about 3½ ounces, of food. The New York State study, with thousands of crops being examined, turned up a record crop with a content of 153 cubic centimeters, almost 5 ounces.

The same study also reported on the amount and the variety of food found in this crop. It contained 188 buds of hop hornbeam, 143 buds of hawthorn, 1 bud of scarlet oak, 223 fruits of staghorn sumac, 37 fruits and seeds of bittersweet, 166 catkins (seed pods) of hop hornbeam, 38 buds of witch hazel, 43 buds of sugar maple, 3 seeds of hawthorn, 696 buds of serviceberry, 2 buds of red cherry, 86 buds of low-bush blueberry, 4 fruits and seeds of maple-leaved viburnum, and leaves of hawkweed, strawberry, and speedwell.

No one should ever have trouble identifying the spot where a ruffed grouse has roosted, particularly in the snow. The droppings are about 1 to 1¼ inches in length and about ⅜ inch in diameter. In the wintertime the droppings will be dark in color and very fibrous because the grouse is feeding on coarse material. In the seasons where green materials, fruit, and berries are eaten, the droppings are still elongated but more formless and often are partially white in color.

*Barberries and staghorn sumac berries are also on the grouse's menu.*

I have found as many as 73 droppings in a single bed, excreted by a single grouse in a single night. (The grouse had roosted in freshly fallen snow, so everything could be verified.) Winter nights are long, so let's figure that the grouse spent twelve hours in that spot. At that rate it would have excreted one dropping every twelve minutes. Without benefit of extensive laboratory tests, just the presence of this many droppings is an indication that the food consumed by that particular grouse was very low in nutritional value. There is one record of 200 droppings in a place where a grouse had burrowed beneath the snow. However, there was no accurate way of telling how long the grouse was under the snow; it might have been several days.

Although I figured that the grouse had spent twelve hours there, it's not really likely. To consume that much food the grouse has to feed longer. It is true that grouse prefer to feed early and late in the day, but in winter they are apt to feed all day and part of the night. I have often found grouse feeding as late as 9 P.M. on cold moonlit nights.

In winter the peak feeding period of the day is 4 P.M. The grouse then literally gorge themselves. Friends of mine, Virginia and Wayne Sharp, of Brookside, New Jersey, have Washington thorn apple trees around their house. Every day about 4 P.M. the grouse come from the woods to feed. The birds walk to the edge of the woods and then fly directly into the trees, which are usually bent down with fruit that lasts most of the winter, providing the grouse with a reliable commissary.

The New York State studies showed that, as the air temperature dropped, the metabolism of the ruffed grouse increased but food passage through the body slowed down, so that all possible nutrients could be absorbed before the waste material was excreted.

Extensive tests showed that an adult ruffed grouse must consume seventy-eight calories per day to maintain its body weight at moderate

*Ruffed grouse droppings: one bird, one night.*

temperatures. As the air temperature dropped, it was found that caloric intake had to be increased. When this was not possible, the birds' weight naturally dropped. Even though some birds were in the process of gaining, their body weight would drop overnight. (All animals that spend the night sleeping, including humans, weigh less in the morning than they did the night before, as no food is ingested and the body burns calories during sleep.)

A hard winter with lots of ice storms can cause a localized grouse decline regardless of the timing of the grouse's ten-year cycle. Males that come through the winter with an excessive weight loss tend to do a lot less drumming and actual mating. Underweight females are less likely to nest; and if they do their clutches of eggs will be smaller, the eggs will have a higher degree of infertility, and the chicks that do hatch will have less stamina.

The overwinter mortality usually runs to 70 percent of the grouse's autumnal population. This reduces the grouse to their lowest yearly figure, but enough survive to reproduce their kind to the extent that the habitat permits.

*131*

*Despite the winter losses, enough grouse survive each year to rebuild their numbers.*

# The Ruffed Grouse
# and Man

THERE HAVE ALWAYS BEEN farseeing people, including so-called "prophets of doom," who decry the way things are going and predict that it will be worse in the future. Today, and with good reason, among such people are found our conservationists and ecologists. The Bible says, "As ye sow, so shall ye reap." The term "plundered planet" is an excellent one to describe our treatment of the earth, but the important thing is that for the first time in the history of mankind there is sufficient interest being shown by enough concerned people that the destruction of our environment may be slowed, perhaps halted, and, we hope, reversed. At last man is actually concerned with the ultimate survival of man, which means the survival also of the myriad forms of life that share this planet with us.

Many are concerned with the future of the ruffed grouse in North America. There are daily newspaper reports of poisonous mercury residues found in pheasants and quail, in fresh- and saltwater fishes, and in various animals. No one yet knows just what these mercury residues will do to wild animals that have ingested it, but we have learned that certain levels of mercury in their body tissues make them dangerous for human consumption. Although some of the mercury was dumped directly into our rivers as a waste product of industrial processes, much of it has been applied to our agricultural lands as a fungicide. Although large numbers of quail and pheasants

*133*

have had access to the mercury used in agriculture, the ruffed grouse, being a forest bird, has not been adversely affected.

The use of the chlorinated hydrocarbon pesticides, such as DDT, dieldrin, and chlordane, has been so widespread that biologists have great difficulty finding any living organism anywhere in the world that does not have accumulated traces of these compounds in its body. Again, the bulk of these pesticides have been used on farmlands, but they were also used on forests to control such tree pests as the gypsy moth and the spruce budworm. There are records of entire broods of ruffed grouse being wiped out by eating larvae of spruce budworm that had been killed by aerial applications of DDT. Fortunately, the further use of hydrocarbons is being strictly controlled or banned outright.*

What is the future for the ruffed grouse population? The answer hinges mainly upon what we do about our own exploding human population. Today, man controls the fate of the wildlife of the world.

The ruffed grouse is considered a forest bird and is never found far from trees. The Indians used the ruffed grouse as a source of food and had little trouble snaring them or shooting them with blunt bird arrows. Woodland Indians were never a deciding factor in the ruffed grouse's population, however, because there never were a great many woodland Indians, and there really weren't a great many ruffed grouse in the virgin woodlands, either.

The Indians used to practice a crude form of game management. They knew that the new growth of plant life that followed a burn created naturally by lightning made excellent food for deer and increased their numbers, so they would often set fire to the forest and burn over large tracts of land. What benefited the deer benefited the ruffed grouse.

---

* On June 13, 1972, William D. Ruckelshaus, Administrator of the Environmental Protection Agency, banned almost all uses of DDT effective December 31, 1972.—*The Editor.*

### The Ruffed Grouse and Man

When the European settlers came, their use of the ax and the torch fostered a tremendous upswing in the numbers of ruffed grouse by destroying the virgin climax forests. Through the 1700s and into the 1800s grouse were found in ever increasing numbers; they probably reached their all-time high sometime after the middle of the last century. Market hunters took a heavy toll of grouse, but their shooting did not cause the numbers of grouse to decline. At the end of the 1800s and the early 1900s the grouse did decline, but this would have happened even without the market hunters, because the brush on abandoned farms had grown into forests that were reaching maturity again.

Throughout these periods of relative scarcity, abundance, and scarcity, the numbers of grouse were following a cycle. The first record that a period of ruffed grouse scarcity was recognized was in 1708 when the colony of New York passed a law closing the season. The province of Quebec, Canada, did the same thing in 1721. The cycle was not understood in those days, however; it is not fully understood today.

In 1830 Thomas Nuttall, a botanist and ornithologist, was returning from an extended plant-collecting trip through Massachusetts and New Hampshire. In that year grouse were so plentiful they could

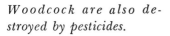

*Woodcock are also de-stroyed by pesticides.*

be purchased in Boston for twelve and a half cents apiece. The following year he made another trip and stated that "while travelling the length of New Hampshire not a single bird of the species [ruffed grouse] was nowhere to be seen."

The best markets for the sale of ruffed grouse were Boston, New York, and Philadelphia. Prices fluctuated according to how many grouse were available, from a low of eight cents per bird up to a high of three dollars and fifty cents. The highest prices were paid after market hunting was abolished in the early 1900s and the birds were sold on the black market.

Market hunters took to the woods from September through December, unless the weather turned exceedingly warm. The grouse were most often shipped to market by railroad, packed in barrels. Refrigeration as such was unknown.

Usually, where a man depended upon hunting for a living, the grouse were taken by any means available. Most, of course, were killed with a shotgun, but many were taken with snares and some with the use of traps, grouse coops, nets, and bird lime. Black-powder hand-loaded shells in a double-barreled 12-gauge shotgun were standard until the Winchester Model 1897 12-gauge pump gun made its debut and reigned supreme in the grouse woods.

The really good market hunters were usually the best wing shots.

*Greenbrier thickets provide food and shelter for grouse.*

They had to be able to produce results and expected to down one bird for every two shells expended. The best shooters would expect to take twenty-five grouse per day, with a top take of perhaps thirty-five. The real pros were also shooting other game that they flushed at the same time. In 1889 a father-and-son team near Ghent, New York, took over one hundred pieces of game in one day. The bag contained rabbits, squirrels, quail, and fifty-two ruffed grouse.

The market hunters never became rich, but they could make more money hunting than they could farming, cutting timber, or whatever they worked at for the rest of the year. These men were not game hogs; they were a product of their time, looked up to and respected by those who knew them. The science of game management was not yet understood.

The low point for almost all wildlife in the United States came in the two decades between 1890 and 1910. The passenger pigeon was gone, the heath hen and the Carolina parakeet virtually so. The bison, antelope, and elk were reduced to mere fractions of their former plentitude. But this era, which took such a toll of our natural resources, also produced men concerned with the future of wildlife. Theodore Roosevelt, Gifford Pinchot, Witmer Stone, William T. Hornaday, Henry Herbert, Spencer Fullerton Baird, John Lacey, and Orverton Price, among others, in their capacities as executives, legislators, naturalists, and educators, made people aware of the plight of remaining wildlife. They set aside preserves, passed laws, made studies, and established conservation as we know it today.

It remained for Aldo Leopold, the father of game management, to develop and expound the ecological interrelationship of wildlife and habitat and of both to man. Leopold's book, *Game Management,* published in 1933, is the foundation for all of the work being done today in that field.

The first game-management procedures were done on a trial-and-error basis. Game management is not an exact science, since it deals with live components. Great progress has been made and general rules can now be applied, but it should never be forgotten that each bird or other animal is an individual.

Leopold found that game management, as practiced in his day by the state game departments, usually followed a set pattern. He listed the sequence as follows:

1. Hunting control
2. Predator control
3. Land reservation
4. Artificial replenishment
5. Environmental control

Hunting control usually meant that hunting was in part forbidden; that for certain times of the year no hunting of a species was allowed. This is still our most commonly used form of control. The length of the ruffed grouse hunting season, for example, has swung from the first limited time restriction on hunting them in New York in 1708 to the first year-round closed season in New Jersey in 1869. Now the pendulum is swinging the other way, as state after state is experimenting with ever-lengthening seasons. Research has proved that if all other factors remain equal the hunting of ruffed grouse does not affect the population.

Alaska's hunting season on the ruffed grouse extends from August until May with a bag limit of fifteen birds per day. True, Alaska's human population is very small. However, in 1869, my own state of New Jersey had a population of 906,069. I don't know what the grouse population was, but it was so low that no hunting of this bird was allowed for three years. One hundred years later, in 1969, our human population had increased to over 9,000,000, making New Jersey the most densely populated state in the nation. I don't know what our ruffed grouse population is today, either; but a couple of years ago the hunting season on ruffed grouse was lengthened from five weeks to three months. (Of course, as we have changed from a rural to an urban society, there are probably fewer hunters per capita today.)

Michigan tried lengthening the season by opening it early, before the grouse dispersal period. More birds were seen, but the foliage was so heavy that the hunters didn't do as well over the longer season as they ordinarily did hunting fewer birds during the regular later season. I don't know who to credit, but this quote sums up the entire situation: "Leaving the season open in poor years will allow the hunters the recreation of carrying a gun afield and won't hurt next year's population a bit."

Second on Leopold's list was predator control. That meant a concerted program to try to eliminate whatever species was thought to be threatening the species that man wanted to save for himself, usually by placing bounties on the predators. The bounty system proved to be fraudulent; it did not achieve predator control but did lead to the destruction of hawks, owls, foxes, weasels, fishers, wolves, skunks, and other predatory animals—all highly useful in maintaining a healthy environment for grouse and other animals—and probably wasted more money than any other game encouragement project so far concocted by well-meaning proponents.*

* The reader is referred in the Bibliography to an excellent treatment of the subject, *Bounties Are Bunk,* by Roger M. Latham of Pennsylvania, whose Game Commission has had a long and historic association with the bounty system.—*The Editor.*

*Two predators: the weasel and the fisher.*

Records also show that on occasion a bounty was placed on grouse to save something else! C. J. Maynard recorded that in 1896 some Massachusetts towns had a twenty-five-cent bounty on ruffed grouse in an effort to reduce so-called damage done by their eating buds of fruit trees. In 1923–1924, the New Hampshire Fish and Game Department paid out almost $25,000 for so-called damage done by grouse to orchards. Yet, Burton L. Spiller, in his book *Grouse Feathers*, reported five grouse ate buds in an apple tree for a period of two weeks, and the tree produced more apples that year than it ever had before. Perhaps the grouse eating buds from the tree produced the same effect as pruning would do, i.e., all possible growth went to the remaining apples. It is true that one grouse may eat 1,300 buds in one day and consume a quarter of a million buds each year. However, as I have already stated, grouse never disbud a branch completely; they move almost constantly while feeding.

Third on the list, land reservation, meant the establishment of refuges, or nonhunting areas; this has been done, is being done, and will continue to be done. With threatened species the refuge is needed to hold the nucleus of the breeding stock. Some species, such as the California condor, have highly specialized survival requirements, and only by making their range a refuge can we hope to hold them back from extinction.

Fourth in Leopold's sequence came artificial replenishment, or the propagation in captivity of different species. This meets with varying degrees of success, according to the species. Artificial propagation is the only hope for survival of many of the world's endangered animals. With some species, such as the ring-necked pheasant or the mallard duck, artificial propagation has enjoyed tremendous success. Many states and private individuals have tried to duplicate these successes with the ruffed grouse. Dr. Arthur A. Allan of Cornell University was one of the first persons to succeed in raising grouse artifically. During the New York State study, large numbers of grouse were so raised.

Michigan has also had good results with raising grouse; with a 77-percent fertility and egg hatch, 76 percent of the birds produced were raised. Both programs proved that ruffed grouse can be raised artifically, but neither could show that it is financially feasible to do so.

Leopold found the last resource to be environmental control, and he summed up his position in his 1929 report to the Committee on American Wild Life Policy when he stated, "If there is any breeding stock at all, the one and only thing we can do to raise a crop of game is to make the environment more favorable."

Under optimum conditions ruffed grouse can repopulate themselves to a maximum density in four breeding seasons. This rapid population buildup is primarily the result of a very high reproductive rate, resulting from sufficient nutritious food and protective cover. One grouse to four acres of land is considered maximum carrying capacity for the best of habitat, because the grouse themselves will not tolerate a higher population.

Walter L. Palmer and G. A. Ammann of Michigan have shown that proper habitat management can help offset the cyclic decline of grouse. This cycle can be delayed, it can be shortened, it is not the same across the nation, it is not the same in the same area, but its existence cannot be denied.

It is interesting to note that when Michigan introduced ruffed grouse to some of its offshore islands, the grouse population exploded regardless of the cycle of the mainland grouse. However, in four years the islands reached their carrying capacity and the grouse went into a cycle identical with those on the mainland.

My personal observations lead me to believe that New Jersey's cycle on grouse should hit its peak in 1972 and 1973. Checking the records of other states I find that most of them seem also to be on a ten-year cycle with peak years ending in the number two and the low years ending in number seven. The grouse in my area have been increasing steadily since 1969.

The easiest part of game management is managing the game; the most difficult is educating the people involved so that the game can be managed. Research has given us the knowledge and the techniques to manage the ruffed grouse, but no state can afford to manage them on a scale large enough to be of much benefit. That is, they cannot afford to manage just the grouse. But the ecological approach, wherein the management of grouse is considered as management of the habitat with its related wildlife as a whole, is possible.

The proper harvesting of deer is good grouse management as well. In Vermont, for example, in recent years the deer herd has far exceeded the carrying capacity of the land, and habitat destruction and winter deer kill are widespread. The destruction of the habitat means a reduction in the population of ruffed grouse because the understory of vegetation that the grouse needs is lacking. Taking more surplus deer by such means as increased doe hunting would benefit the deer, the habitat, *and* the grouse, but Vermont refuses to permit its game managers to practice good deer management.

For years the aspen has been considered to be a "weed" tree. Now new methods of pulping have turned it into a valuable resource. Clear-cutting is the most economical way to harvest the aspen but also the most destructive. Systematic block cutting would still take all

*Young aspens are no longer considered "weed" trees.*

of the desired trees but would not exterminate the wildlife living in the forest. As blocks of aspen were harvested at different times, the regeneration of the forest would allow for the varied stages of growth that would benefit all kinds of wildlife. We have the tools and we have the knowledge for good game management; all we need now is the education to make such management possible.

The ruffed grouse has encountered man, from his very beginning here in North America, and has survived in spite of all man has done or attempted to do. It has not succumbed to man's persecution and takes little note of his blandishments. The king of the game birds, the grouse needs only suitable habitat to be able to maintain its own. With modern man's interest in ecology and in saving as much of our natural world as is possible, the future of the ruffed grouse seems to be assured. "Long live the king."

*Long live the king.*

# Subspecies of the Ruffed Grouse

As WE SAW in the opening chapter, the first ruffed grouse from North America was called *Tetrao umbellus* by Linnaeus, the *Tetrao* lumping this new grouse with the better-known European one. J. F. Stephens was the first to suggest that the name *Tetrao* be changed to *Bonasa,* but he failed to say whether he was referring to the ruffed grouse or the heath hen. In 1840 G. R. Gray settled the matter by designating *Bonasa* as the generic name for the ruffed grouse.

There have been numerous changes in the subspecies, but the American Ornithologists' Union's *Check-List of North American Birds* for 1957 recognizes ten.*

Differences in colors, for example, are common to a greater or lesser degree in most of the subspecies, which range from a deep russet red through pale buff and light gray to a deep charcoal gray.

---

* Each species or "kind" of bird, such as the ruffed grouse itself, has a certain species form (or outline), physical characteristics, and, usually, a biology and life habits that markedly distinguish it from other species, even its closest relatives. For example, few people looking at a ruffed grouse, a related prairie chicken, and a sharp-tailed grouse would have difficulty telling them apart. Some bird species, however—and this includes the ruffed grouse—while typical of their kind in many ways, show marked variations in different parts of their overall range. These geographical varieties, usually distinguishable only by the scientists who study them, are the subspecies or races that have evolved in response to the regional or even local climate and environment over a long period of time. The ruffed grouse is a species, but all of its representatives are local or geographical ones, called subspecies.—*The Editor.*

145

This makes identification of the subspecies of the ruffed grouse by color very difficult.

1. *Bonasa umbellus umbellus,* the eastern ruffed grouse and the so-called nominate subspecies, lives from east-central Minnesota, southern Wisconsin, and southwestern Michigan south to central Arkansas, western Tennessee, western Kentucky, and central Indiana, and from central New York and Massachusetts south to eastern Pennsylvania, eastern Maryland, and New Jersey to central Virginia.

2. *Bonasa umbellus togata,* the Canada ruffed grouse, is a little larger and heavier than the eastern ruffed grouse and is usually grayer. It ranges from northeastern Minnesota, southern Ontario and Quebec, New Brunswick, and Nova Scotia south to northern Wisconsin, central Michigan, southeastern Ontario, central New York, western and northern Massachusetts, and northwestern Connecticut.

3. *Bonasa umbellus monticola,* the Appalachian ruffed grouse, is slightly more rufous than the Canada ruffed grouse. It ranges from southeastern Michigan, northeastern Ohio, and the western half of Pennsylvania south to northern Georgia, northwestern South Carolina, western North Carolina, and the mountain and piedmont areas of western Virginia and Maryland.

4. *Bonasa umbellus incana,* the hoary ruffed grouse, is an ashy-colored grouse residing in southeastern Idaho, central-western Wyoming, and northeastern North Dakota south to central Utah, northwestern Colorado, and western South Dakota.

5. *Bonasa umbellus umbelloides,* the gray ruffed grouse, is a light-gray- to slate-gray-colored bird with only occasionally a little brown occurring on the ruff and tail. This grouse has the largest range of the species, covering an area from extreme southeastern Alaska, northern British Columbia, north-central Alberta, central Saskatchewan, central Manitoba, northern Ontario, and central Quebec south, east of the coastal ranges and the Cascades to southern British Columbia, western Montana, southeastern Idaho, extreme northwestern

Bonasa umbellus umbellus.

Wyoming, southern Saskatchewan, southern Manitoba, southern Ontario, and across south-central Quebec to the north shore of the Gulf of St. Lawrence to southeastern Labrador.

6. *Bonasa umbellus phaia,* the Idaho ruffed grouse, lives from southeastern British Columbia, eastern Washington, and northern Idaho south to eastern Oregon and on the western slopes of the Rocky Mountains to south-central Idaho.

7. *Bonasa umbellus brunnescens,* the Vancouver Island ruffed grouse, has a range restricted to the island whose name it bears and to some of the adjoining islands in British Columbia.

8. *Bonasa umbellus yukonensis,* the Yukon ruffed grouse, is the largest and the grayest of all the subspecies. It lives from western Alaska to the east, chiefly in the valleys of the Yukon and Kuskokwim rivers, and across the central Yukon to northern Alberta and northwestern Saskatchewan.

9. *Bonasa umbellus sabini,* the Oregon ruffed grouse (first seen by Lewis and Clark in 1805), is a large, very dark-brown grouse that lives west of the Rocky Mountains from southwestern British Columbia south through western-central Washington, Oregon, and northwestern California.

10. *Bonasa umbellus castanea,* the Olympic ruffed grouse, is the darkest of all the rufous-colored grouse; no gray phase is known. Its range extends from the Olympic Peninsula and the shores of Puget Sound south through western Washington to the mouth of the Columbia River.

Two organizations created for the purpose of disseminating the latest information about the ruffed grouse are The Ruffed Grouse Society of America at Alexandria, Virginia, and Grouse Cover at Jeannette, Pennsylvania.

# Bibliography

Allen, Durward L. *Our Wildlife Legacy.* New York: Funk and Wagnalls Co., 1954.

Allison, Donald G. "Basic Features of the New Hampshire Ruffed Grouse Census," *Journal of Wildlife Management,* vol. 27, no. 4 (October 1963).

————. *Factors Affecting Grouse Population Changes.* New Hampshire Investigation Reports, 1959–1962.

American Ornithologists' Union. *Check-List of North American Birds.* 5th edition. Lancaster, Pa.: American Ornithologists' Union, 1957.

Ammann, G. A. "Public Acceptance of the December 1964 Grouse Season in Zone Three," Information Circular no. 141, Michigan Department of Conservation (July 1965).

————. *Ten Facts About Ruffed Grouse.* Report no. 2386, Michigan Department of Conservation (August 1962).

————, and L. A. Ryel. "Extensive Methods of Inventorying Ruffed Grouse in Michigan," *Journal of Wildlife Management,* vol. 27, no. 4 (October 1963).

Baillie, J. L. *Ontario Grouse.* Royal Ontario Museum Division of Zoology, November 1956.

Bakeless, John. *The Eyes of Discovery.* New York: Dover Publications, Inc., 1961.

Bent, Arthur C. *Life Histories of North American Gallinaceous Birds.* New York: Dover Publications, Inc., 1963.

Berner, Alfred, and Leslie W. Gysel. "Habitat Analysis and Management Considerations for Ruffed Grouse for a Multiple Use Area in Michigan," *Journal of Wildlife Management,* vol. 33, no. 4 (October 1969).

Boag, D. A., and K. M. Sumanik. "Characteristics of Drumming Sites Selected by Ruffed Grouse in Alberta," *Journal of Wildlife Management,* vol. 33, no. 3 (July 1969).

Brown, Thomas E. "Compatibility of Deer and Grouse," *New York Fish and Game Journal,* Conservation Department, Albany, New York, July 1964.

Bump, Gardiner, Robert W. Darrow, Frank C. Edminster, and Walter F. Crissey. "The Ruffed Grouse," New York State Department of Conservation, Albany, New York, 1947.

Buyukmihci, Hope Sawyer. "A Date with the Drum-m-m-e-r-r," *Audubon Magazine,* March-April 1967.

Camp, Raymond R., ed. *The Hunter's Encyclopedia.* Harrisburg, Pa.: The Stackpole Co., 1957.

Carson, Rachel. *Silent Spring.* Boston: Houghton Mifflin Co., 1962.

Chambers, Robert E., and Ward M. Sharp. "Movement and Dispersal Within a Population of Ruffed Grouse," *Journal of Wildlife Management,* vol. 22, no. 3 (July 1958).

Chapman, Floyd B., Hubert Bezdek, and Eugene H. Dustman. "The Ruffed Grouse and Its Management in Ohio," Wildlife Conservation Bulletin no. 6, Columbus, Ohio, November 1948.

Cliff, Edward P. *Wildlife Habitat Improvement Handbook* (FSH 2609.11). Washington, D.C.: U.S. Department of Agriculture, 1969.

Cringan, A. T. "Reproductive Biology of Ruffed Grouse in Southern Ontario 1964–68," *Journal of Wildlife Management,* vol. 34, no. 4 (October 1970).

Davis, Jeffrey A. "Aging and Sexing Criteria for Ohio Ruffed Grouse," *Journal of Wildlife Management,* vol. 33, no. 3 (July 1969).

Dorney, Robert S. "Sex and Age Structure of Wisconsin Ruffed Grouse Populations," *Journal of Wildlife Management,* vol. 27, no. 4 (October 1963).

———, and Helmer M. Mattison. "Trapping Techniques for Ruffed Grouse," *Journal of Wildlife Management,* vol. 20, no. 1 (January 1956).

*Bibliography*

Duvendeck, Jerry P. *The 1966 Extended Ruffed Grouse Hunting Season on Garden and High Islands.* Report no. 117, Michigan Department of Conservation, July 1967.

Edminster, Frank C. *The Ruffed Grouse.* New York: The Macmillan Co., 1947.

Elton, Charles. *Voles, Mice and Lemmings.* London: Oxford University Clarendon Press, 1942.

Errington, Paul L. *Of Predation and Life.* Ames, Iowa: Iowa State University Press, 1967.

Evanoff, Vlad, ed. *Hunting Secrets of the Experts.* New York: Doubleday and Co., Inc., 1964.

Evans, George B. "Bird in Hand," *Pennsylvania Game News,* July 1967.

Everett, Fred. *Fun With Game Birds.* Harrisburg, Pa.: The Stackpole Co., 1954.

Fay, L. Dale. "Recent Success in Raising Ruffed Grouse in Captivity," *Journal of Wildlife Management,* vol. 27, no. 4 (October 1963).

Godfrey, Geoffrey A., and William H. Marshall. "Brood Break-up and Dispersal of Ruffed Grouse," *Journal of Wildlife Management,* vol. 33, no. 3 (July 1969).

Godfrey, Joe, Jr., and Frank Dufresne. *The Great Outdoors.* New York: McGraw-Hill Book Co., Inc., 1947.

Grange, Wallace B. *The Way to Game Abundance.* New York: Charles Scribner's Sons, 1949.

————. *Wisconsin Grouse Problems.* Wisconsin Conservation Department, Madison, Wis., 1948.

Greene, Robert G., and J. E. Schillinger. "A Natural Infection of Sharp-Tail Grouse and the Ruffed Grouse by *Pastuella Tularense,*" *Proceedings of the Society of Experimental Biology and Medicine,* vol. 30, 284–287.

Gullion, Gordon W. "Stopping the Decline and Fall of Grouse," *Field and Stream Magazine,* December 1970.

————, and William H. Marshall. *Survival of Ruffed Grouse in a Boreal Forest.* Seventh Annual, Cornell Laboratory of Ornithology, Ithaca, New York, 1968.

Hale, James B., and Robert S. Dorney. "Seasonal Movements of Ruffed

Grouse in Wisconsin," *Journal of Wildlife Management,* vol. 27, no. 4 (October 1963).

Hall, Henry Marion. *The Ruffed Grouse.* New York: Oxford University Press, 1946.

Hazel, Robert. *Management of the Ruffed Grouse in North Carolina.* North Carolina Resources Commission, Raleigh, N.C., May 1953.

Herbert, Henry William. *Frank Forester's Field Sports.* Vol. 1. New York: Stringer and Townsend, 1848.

Hosley, N. W. *Ruffed Grouse Range Improvement in Central New Hampshire.* New Hampshire Fish and Game Department, August 1940.

Howell, F. Clark. *Early Man.* New York: Time Inc., 1965.

Johnson, George. *Ruffed Grouse and Wild Turkey Investigation.* Wildlife Research Report, vol. 26, no. 2, Indiana Department of Natural Resources, 1965.

————. *Ruffed Grouse Nesting Study.* Wildlife Research Report, vol. 27, no. 1, Indiana Department of Natural Resources, 1966.

Keith, Lloyd B. *Wildlife's Ten-Year Cycle.* Madison, Wis.: University of Wisconsin Press, 1963.

King, Ralph T. "Ruffed Grouse Management," *Roosevelt Wildlife Bulletin,* vol. 8, no. 3 (Syracuse University, N.Y., 1943).

Knight, John Alden. *Ruffed Grouse.* New York: Alfred A. Knopf, 1947.

Knowlton, Robert B., Harold W. Pillsbury, Sumner A. Dole, Jr., and Arthur E. MacGregor. *Summary of Grouse Crop and Gizzard Analysis for 1940.* Technical Circular no. 9, New Hampshire Fish and Game Department, 1940.

Koller, Larry. *The Treasury of Hunting.* New York: Ridge Press, Inc., Odyssey Press Inc., 1965.

Lane, Frank W. *Animal Wonder World.* New York: Sheridan House, 1951.

Latham, Roger M. *Bounties Are Bunk,* National Wildlife Federation Leaflet, Washington, D.C., 1960.

Leopold, Aldo. *Game Management.* New York: Charles Scribner's Sons, 1933.

Madson, John. *Ruffed Grouse.* East Alton, Ill.: Winchester Press, 1969.

Marshall, William H. "Ruffed Grouse and Snowshoe Hare Populations," *Journal of Wildlife Management,* vol. 18, no. 1 (January 1954).

Martin, Alexander C., Herbert S. Zim, and Arnold L. Nelson. *American Wildlife and Plants: A Guide to Wildlife Food Habits.* New York: McGraw-Hill Book Co., Inc., 1951.

Martin, John Stuart. "Sam Grouse of the Jenny Jump," personal correspondence, not dated but about 1962.

Moran, Richard J., and Walter L. Palmer. "Ruffed Grouse Introductions and Population Trends on Michigan Islands," *Journal of Wildlife Management,* vol. 27, no. 4 (October 1963).

Mosby, Henry S., ed. *Wildlife Investigational Techniques.* Washington, D.C.: The Wildlife Society, 1963.

Neave, David J., and Bruce S. Wright. "The Effects of Weather and D.D.T. Spraying on a Ruffed Grouse Population," *Journal of Wildlife Management,* vol. 33, no. 4 (October 1969).

Nelson, A. L., Talbott E. Clarke, and W. W. Bailey. *Early Winter Food of Ruffed Grouse on the George Washington National Forest.* Circular no. 504, U.S. Department of Agriculture, Washington, D.C. (December 1938).

Norris, Charles C. *Eastern Upland Shooting.* Philadelphia: J. B. Lippincott Co., 1946.

Palmer, Walter L. "Ruffed Grouse Drumming Sites in Northern Michigan," *Journal of Wildlife Management,* vol. 27, no. 4 (October 1963).

———. "Ruffed Grouse Flight Capability Over Water," *Journal of Wildlife Management,* vol. 26, no. 3 (July 1962).

———. *Sexing Live-Trapped Juvenile Ruffed Grouse,* Report no. 2154, Michigan Department of Conservation (December 1957).

———, and G. A. Ammann. *Ruffed Grouse and Woodcock Populations on Several Small Study Units of the Gratiot-Saginaw State Game Area.* Report no. 136, Michigan Department of Conservation, February 1968.

———, and Carl L. Bennett, Jr. "Relation of Season Length to Hunting Harvest of Ruffed Grouse," *Journal of Wildlife Management,* vol. 27, no. 4 (October 1963).

Pearson, T. Gilbert, ed. *Birds of America.* Garden City, N.Y.: Garden

City Publishing Co., Inc., 1917.

Prawdzik, Thomas R. "Ruffed Grouse Escaping a Cooper's Hawk," *Journal of Wildlife Management,* vol. 27, no. 4 (October 1963).

Reed, Chester A. *North American Birds' Eggs.* New York: Dover Publications, Inc., 1965.

Ritcey, R. W., and R. Y. Edwards. "Grouse Abundance and June Temperatures in Wells Gray Park, British Columbia," *Journal of Wildlife Management,* vol. 27, no. 4 (October 1963).

Robinson, Ben C. *Woodland, Field and Waterfowl Hunting.* Philadelphia: David McKay Co., 1946.

Sawyer, Edmund J. "The Ruffed Grouse with Special Reference to Its Drumming," *Roosevelt Wildlife Bulletin,* vol. 1, no. 3 (Syracuse University, 1923).

————. Personal correspondence on ruffed grouse, January 1970.

Sharp, Ward M. "The Effects of Habitat Manipulation and Forest Succession on Ruffed Grouse," *Journal of Wildlife Management,* vol. 27, no. 4 (October 1963).

Shelford, Victor E. *The Ecology of North America.* Urbana, Ill.: University of Illinois Press, 1963.

Shimmel, Albert G. "Observations from the Drumming Log," *Virginia Wildlife Magazine,* February 1968.

Siegler, Hilbert R. *New Hampshire Nature Notes.* Oxford, N.H.: Equity Publishing Corp., 1962.

Smith, Ned. "Who Needs a Grouse Dog?" *Outdoor Life Magazine,* October 1965.

Spiller, Burton L. *Grouse Feathers.* The Derrydale Press, 1935.

Terres, John K. *The Wonders I See.* Philadelphia: J. B. Lippincott Co., 1960.

Trefethen, James B. *Wildlife Management and Conservation.* Boston: D. C. Heath and Co., 1964.

Trippensee, Reuben Edwin. *Wildlife Management,* vol. 1. New York: McGraw-Hill Book Co., Inc., 1948.

VanTyne, Josselyn, and Andrew J. Berger. *Fundamentals of Ornithology.* New York: John Wiley and Sons, Inc., 1965.

Woolner, Frank. *Grouse and Grouse Hunting.* New York: Crown Publishers, Inc., 1970.

# Index

*Italic page numbers indicate illustrations.*

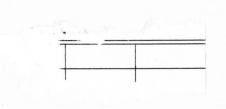